Students and

TIME & AGAIN

HELEN THOMAS
TIME & AGAIN
memoirs and letters

edited by Myfanwy Thomas

Carcanet · Manchester

First published in 1978 by
Carcanet New Press Limited
330 Corn Exchange Buildings
Manchester M4 3BG

Carcanet New Press Limited acknowledges the financial
assistance of the Arts Council of Great Britain.

Printed in Great Britain by offset lithography by
Billing & Sons Ltd, Guildford, London and Worcester

CONTENTS

PHOTOGRAPH ALBUM

I / NELLIE NOBLE: EARLY DAYS

VERY EARLY DAYS

I WAS BORN in Liverpool on 11 July 1877. I remember nothing of this period, but my mother has told me that when I was still a baby and the youngest of the family, having a brother Philip two years older and a sister Irene four years older, our neighbourhood was stricken by a terrible epidemic of diphtheria. At that time there was no cure and my brother Philip, a cousin and an aunt all died of it. I had it but recovered. My mother related how no one would call at the house and she had to do her shopping by night, going to the back doors of the shops. Many children and adults in the neighbourhood served by the same milkman—for it was contaminated milk that caused the disease—died; and I expect that it was owing to these deaths that my parents moved to Ainsdale when I was about three.

At this little village among the sandhills my first memories begin. I remember vaguely the sandy unpaved village street into which my bare toes sank. I remember very vividly being bathed in a tin bath in front of the kitchen fire, and how, the nurse being called away, I darted out of the door and ran, all naked and wet as I was, down the village street to the house of a beloved relative whom I knew as Cousin Robert, and I remember his wrapping me in a blanket and being carried in his arms, my toes getting entangled in his beard.

One other memory of this time I have of being carried on my father's shoulders, astride his neck and clasping his forehead. He was very tall and the height I was at seemed to be immense. I can still feel the shudder of dizziness as he strode along to the village green, where he set me down, spreading his coat for me to sit on, while he joined a group of men to play quoits. I can hear the ring of the heavy iron quoits.

No other memory of this period is retained, not even of my mother and only the tallness of my father. It was at this remote village that my younger sister Mary, born I think at Ainsdale, was stolen by gipsies. My elder sister Irene, then aged about seven, had the baby in charge. Mary was a pretty fair-haired child and the gipsies took a fancy to her and offered Irene a gaily coloured necklace in exchange for her, which Irene readily accepted. Some hours later the police rescued the child. All this I was told—I have no recollection of the consternation and despair my parents for a few hours endured.

It must have been when I was about five that we moved to London, but of the upheaval of this move I have no memory. We went to live in a street of semi-detached houses near Wandsworth Common. Our road was the last before the open country, and our back garden looked over meadows and an orchard. At the top of our road ran a real country lane, with hedgerows on each side and often very muddy and rough, with deep cart-wheel ruts. This lane was forbidden to us as being the haunt of gipsies, and my parents having had a practical demonstration of their child-stealing ways, feared them. But once, taken by my elder sister, we did venture into the forbidden lane to pick blackberries and were scared by some gipsy children who demanded our berries, which we gave them and ran home as quickly as we could.

My elder sister Irene was always one by herself. Wilful and domineering, she seemed from a very early age to be of a different and superior calibre from myself and her ways did not impinge at all on mine. I and my sister Mary were always referred to as 'the children' and we lived our lives together. We went hand in hand to a little kindergarten school held in the same road and only a few doors away. We were told to remember the house as being next door to the one with a canary in a cage in the window. Mary and I—being the youngest and smallest in the school—were called by the teacher 'the threepenny bits'.

Here we learned to make coloured mats by threading narrow strips of paper into a slotted square, and to model in clay—not the plasticene of later years, but wet grey clay. We also learned to spell from words written on the blackboard. I remember being shocked to see the teacher writing B-O-T among the pots, cots, gots and tots. It was at this time I became aware that I could not see as well as the other children, but had to sit in front of the class, greatly to my embarrassment. We also had slates on which, with our fingers, we made islands and bays and peninsulas in the sand sprinkled on for this purpose. All this I enjoyed and used to take home the work of my hands with pride to show my parents. I also remember the humiliation of being sent home, having wetted my drawers, and the agony of tears when I had to confess to my mother.

A few more memories of this time flit across my mind. Irene gave me a paint box and a copy of the *Illustrated London News* to paint. I chose a full page picture called 'Over the garden wall'. It depicted a capped and beribboned housemaid flirting with a soldier, one each side of a garden wall. I had never used paints before and had not an idea of how to do so. I covered my brush with emerald green paint and smeared it all over the picture, which evoked the mocking laughter of Irene and my tears.

At this house my brother was born and I remember being taken by father to see him and my mother in bed together, and my thinking, 'How lucky that mama is in bed so that she can cuddle the baby.' My parents were delighted at the birth of a son and he was named Lancelot. He does not figure largely in my childhood. But I remember that on his third birthday he was promoted from frocks and petticoats to a sailor suit and that papa was cross when somebody seeing him in his male attire said, 'Oh, I always thought he was a little girl'.

I remember being taken with Mary to be photographed and the little bird we were promised to see. Also that we were given a skipping-rope to hold draped over our laps and that I wanted to take it home and cried when I was told I could not. I have this photograph of one very fair and one very dark little girl, both with their hair cut with a straight fringe over their brows and quite short over the ears. We wore crimson velvet dresses. Behind the photograph in its small velvet frame I found a slip of paper on which is written in my firm hand:

> All that we are we were,
> So different dark and fair,
> The same in this we prove
> Sisters who through life, love.

I think it must have been about this time that Mary and I made a prolonged visit to some rich friends. It may have been that my father was suffering from one of his mysterious periods of paralysis. I have no recollection of this illness of my father's, but my mother has told me how she used to take down from my father's dictation his literary work, and I can well imagine that we were sent away while she coped with the new baby Lancelot and my father's work, which was what we depended on. She told me in later years that Edward Hutton, the editor of *The Spectator*, one of the journals for which my father wrote, and other literary friends, all contributed to the fee of a great nerve specialist who came to see my father. He said my father could not live for more than six months. When mother handed him the cheque for 150 guineas, he handed it back to her. He was quite wrong in his diagnosis as my father recovered and lived many years.

My parents used to attend a Congregational Chapel in Buckingham Palace Road. The minister was a John Simon and must have been an exceptional preacher, for he drew a large congregation from many different parts of London, among whom were a coterie of literary people and those interested in the arts. Among these were the de Selincourts, rich silk merchants, but with many interests in common with my parents with whom they became intimate friends. They came with their large family of children, as did my parents. Basil de Selincourt and I became shy friends. I remember my birthday occurring on a Sunday, and Basil bringing my present to Chapel. It was a box of coloured bricks. This weekly trek of the family to our place of worship was an undertaking that parents would not consider nowadays. It was a good walk to Clapham Junction station from our house, and from Victoria a walk of about ten minutes to the Chapel. But we children sat out the service with good behaviour. Indeed nothing else would have been tolerated by our parents, for however bored the younger children may have been, we were self-controlled and obedient.

The de Selincourts, who took Mary and me off my mother's hands during my father's illness, lived in a large country house standing in a small park and called Wandsworth Lodge. Their children were kept strictly to the nursery or in the garden, in the charge of a nurse. In the grounds was a pond and I remember being scolded by the nurse for getting wet and muddy in the company of Basil. The youngest of the family was Hugh and he was referred to by the nurse as

'Master Baby'. There were many elder children, awe-inspiring grown-ups to me, and when one of them—Muriel—asked me if I was ticklish I did not know what the word meant; when she laughed at my ignorance, I burst into tears.

In the evening, dressed in our best frocks of green velvet, we were taken down to the great dining room to have dessert. I recall my shame at letting some grape juice dribble on to my dress. In the billiards room was a very large dolls' house, a complete replica of Wandsworth Lodge, with the staircase leading to the gallery above the hall and everything in miniature. I had never seen a dolls' house before and I was allowed to play with it.

How long Mary and I were with these kind people I do not know, but it must have been shortly after this that we left London for Lancashire.

SOUTHPORT

I WAS A delicate child, prone to asthma and croup. One of my earliest recollections is waking up in my cot—which was in my parents' bedroom—and clinging to the bars of it, struggling to get my breath, of being lifted out and plunged into a bath of hot water and given ipecacuanha wine to make me sick.

My father was helpless, I was ill, and my brother was still an infant when we left London. We travelled in an invalid saloon. Papa lay on the bed, I was on the sofa and my baby brother in his cot, my mother ministering to us all. Adjoining the saloon was a lavatory for our use. I don't know how long the journey took nor the details of it. But the next thing that impressed itself on my mind is the tall house we found ourselves in. We were in Southport and almost as soon as we were settled in this furnished house, we children fell ill with measles and then mumps. The large drawing room on the first floor was turned into a sick room and here we were looked after by a nurse whose name was Christina. The room had large bay windows and from here I saw papa's first attempts at walking again. A man named Rogers used to come every day and take him out in a bath-chair and it was Rogers who supported and encouraged papa to walk. Rogers was a great favourite with us children and would bring us bags of sea shells and many other playthings.

I first saw the sea during this time and was disappointed with the great featureless stretch of water. I had imagined it as being full of shipping as in a steel engraving that hung on our wall, depicting sailing ships, steamers, tugs, rowing-boats and all the life and movement of a harbour. The sea which confronted me lacked even one ship. The sands at Southport however were full of interest, for they were covered with a wonderful variety of shells, from tiny pink scallop-shaped shells, to long ivory-coloured razor shells, cockle and oyster and convoluted shells. We never tired of collecting these and Christina taught us how to gum them on to cardboard boxes as presents for mother and father. On the beach there were donkeys we could ride and best of all the Punch and Judy show. We were forbidden the ice-cream, called hokey-pokey, as mother knew that the Italian ice-cream man kept his wares under his bed! These days at the beach were rare as mother would not allow us to be among crowds and even in those days, trippers came to Southport.

I suppose it was owing to my father's recovery from his paralysis that we left the furnished lodgings and took an unfurnished house in Southport, and here I had my tenth birthday. This was memorable to me because it happened on a Sunday and I took my presents—one of which was a work-basket, fitted with scissors, thimble, needles and embroidery silks—to show my maternal Grandmother—Grandmama Lunt. This old lady we feared. She was thin and sharp-featured and harsh-tongued. When I asked her if she would like to see my work-basket, she said, 'Certainly not. We don't even *talk* about work-baskets on the Sabbath'. So I put my presents aside and became silent and resentful.

Grandmama Lunt was a strict Calvinist and no frivolity was allowed in her presence. I could not understand how it was that my grandfather—a jolly old sailor—had fallen in love with her, for I could not imagine that she had ever been pretty or kind. But he had been expelled from the Quaker community for marrying outside it, for Grandmama was a Methodist. However, her stern ways and her complete lack of humour may have accounted for Grandpapa's very long absences at sea on a whaling ship, for I was told that he was away for so many years on one voyage without communicating with his wife (indeed I expect that this was almost impossible) that she was allowed to presume his death and marry again if she liked. However, he turned up again and for us children he was the true sailor, with stubbly whiskers, wearing always a blue seaman's jersey and gold rings in his ears, full of yarns and fun and very affectionate to his grandchildren. Now retired, he took the pennies at the turnstile on the pier and would let us through without paying, after first pretending he didn't recognize us.

I have a vivid recollection of Grandmama's sitting room with the heavily carved oak settle and bureau, shining and dark with years and years of polishing with turpentine and beeswax. On the beam over the fireplace hung a bronze plaque, a replica of Leonardo's 'Last Supper'. This I coveted and was the only thing belonging to Grandmama that I liked. With her lived her sister, my Aunt Lily, a kinder but not less fanatical Sabbatarian.

When I was older I learned that when my Lunt grandparents were first married, Grandmama decided to accompany her husband on one of his whaling trips. Grandpapa knew that at one of the Pacific islands they would be royally entertained by the chief of the tribe. In order that his young and puritanical wife should not be shocked, he secretly provided several pairs of striped bathing-drawers for the mother-naked natives. These he managed to get to them before the festivities began. When the guests were all seated round the blazing fire, the festal procession appeared, and each tall shining black man held his head proudly beneath his high blue and white striped turban.

Occasionally Grandmama stayed with us and I had to share her bedroom. My sensibilities were shocked to see her, a voluminous white calico nightgown over her clothes, preparatory to undressing, detaching a long grey switch of hair from beneath her cap and hanging it on the gas bracket. What else, I thought in terror, might she take off and hang up. The most shocking horror was to see her soaking the black skeins of knitting wool—she was always knitting black woollen stockings—in the chamber pot, where the coils lay soggily overnight, haunting my darkness.

A NORTH COUNTRY HOUSEHOLD

ON LOOKING back, what strikes me at once is the wide street on which our house stood. The only traffic on the road were the tradesmen's carts, an occasional trap and the doctor's brougham; the sound of their horses' hoofs and of the wheels was deadened by the slight covering of sand which lay over all flat surfaces. For between us and the sea was a region of sandhills from which the sand continually blew over everything. The pavements were wide and flagged and here we—my sister Mary and I—bowled our wooden hoops, or skipped or pushed our dolls' prams. The boys played with peg tops and marbles. All was safe and peaceful.

Our new house—a largish Victorian villa—was just outside Southport in Birkdale which is now a fashionable golfing place but was then a small suburb of Southport which we children could reach by railway, if we liked, for a penny return.

The house had a garden at the front and back. But in the front, instead of flowers, there was on each side of the path a bank set with huge glistening stones, stark and bare, but very special, I was told, and brought all the way from Derbyshire. Detached and comfortable-looking, the house had large bow windows on either side of the door. The window on the right was the dining-room and on the left the drawing-room, which was hardly ever used except as a playroom for us children, because my father's study on the first floor above the dining-room, a large room lined with books, was also the general sitting-room. Even these windows, in stormy weather, were dimmed by sand which the window-cleaner used to wash off with a hose. This was a great day for us children, for we loved to press our faces against the glass inside the house, while the good-natured man would make us shriek with delight by hosing our faces.

If the afternoons were too wet or cold for our walk with mother, we would sit in father's study on little stools with some childish sewing of dolls' clothes. While we were busy she read aloud to us—Dickens or Wilkie Collins or a fairy story of Hans Andersen or some of Tennyson's poetry. Thus when very small children we came to know and love some of the great literature of England. If Mother grew tired or had

19

other things to do, Father would take the book. These sessions were our greatest delight.

On the floor above the study and four other rooms, mostly bedrooms, were two attic rooms where I and my younger sister slept, and also our maids, Annie and Fanny Wild, two sisters who were with us for years. There was a large landing where we kept our dolls and their cradles and a toy cooking stove where, over a candle, we melted sweets and fried all sorts of odds and ends for our dolls. We played here for hours, lost to all else but our make-believe.

Often there were terrible storms on the coast; gales tore roofs off houses and we would hear the maroon summoning the lifeboat crew to some ship in distress. As the storm roared about our attic we lay and trembled in bed, but having said our prayers, we felt comforted and safe.

Books played a great part in our lives, for the house was full of them. My father reviewed books for several literary journals and though his work was mostly with novels and essays, we had a fine library. Mrs Molesworth, Mrs Ewing, Mrs Hodgson Burnett—we adored *Little Lord Fauntleroy*— Lewis Carroll, the Andrew Lang fairy books and many others came our way.

We began at a penny a week for pocket money and what a variety of things there was to spend it on. You could have twenty-four aniseed balls, brown and hard, changing colour every time you took them out of your mouth and looked at them: it took a long time to reduce them to small white pills. We were forbidden the liquorice bootlaces, ten a penny, as Mother told us they were made of ox's blood from the slaughter-house, and I have never eaten liquorice since that time. There were locust-beans too, unattractive crinkled brown pods, tasting like dry and fibrous dates, the sweetness soon cloying, an experiment not repeated. Penny bazaars there were where you could buy little Japanese fans, tiny soft dolls with china head, hands and feet and a mop of black china curls. A bunch of six slate pencils each wrapped with pretty paper to hold, or a wooden lead pencil with a peep-hole at the top through which you could see a view of Southport. Fragile coloured glass bangles and packets of gay beads to thread. Useful things too—a design on a card pricked with holes and a skein of silk to embroider it with. The choice was endless. But most wonderful of all we could take a return ticket to Southport on the railway for a penny and go on the pier for nothing but a smile to Grandpapa Lunt at the turnstile.

We were not rich or poor, but we lived very simple lives and were pleased with little things. We had no luxuries and hardly any activities outside our home. We went to church and Sunday school and at the latter I vividly remember being given a picture of a yellowhammer. I found the identical yellowhammer in a Victorian scrap-book I was given recently. I was a town child and knew nothing of nature, and this bright bird evoked my longing for the country.

My mother was strict in her training of us, and in our love for her was a grain of fear. When we disobeyed her or broke a rule we knew the punishment would come. We were sent to our rooms, or even to bed, and on rare occasions we were spanked with Mother's slipper. This was the most dreadful thing that could happen, but forgiveness at once followed our repentance. If Mother would not let us have or do something, we would go to Father and he would appeal to Mother—'Oh Essie, let the poor little lambs have it!'—and I fear we traded on his soft heart.

We were allowed to go with other children to play in the sandhills. This was a great treat. The range of dunes stretched as far as the eye could see. The hills varied in height and we climbed up them finding the going difficult in the soft sand, or ran down them into the little valleys very often filled with water, where the lovely Grass of Parnassus grew, Wintergreen and other beautiful flowers. There was a sinister quality about parts of the sandhills, for mad dogs, then not uncommon, found their way there to die or be hunted by men with guns.

My mother was not a hard task-mistress to her two maids, Annie and Fanny, but everything had to be done perfectly, and though she would allow no shirking of the work, her maids stayed with her for a long time. I can see her now coming in at the front door into the wide hall and bending down to look along the top of the table to see if it had been dusted, and any omission of their duties mother immediately pointed out to Annie her housemaid or to Fanny her cook.

21

Annie, the younger of the two, earned fourteen pounds a year and her sister Fanny sixteen pounds, rising by small increases each year. They kept our house of ten rooms in perfect order and Mother praised good work as well as complaining of bad. They both dressed, in the mornings, in pretty pink or mauve print dresses and plain white aprons, which they made themselves, and little starched caps. In the afternoons, black dresses with beribboned caps and frilly aprons were worn.

The kitchen, which was their domain, was behind the dining-room, looking on to the back garden. Out of this led a large scullery with a huge stone sink, and out of that a large larder or pantry as it was called in the north. Kitchen, scullery and larder all had stone-flagged floors which it was Fanny's duty to keep clean. The kitchen had mats on the floor as well for comfort and warmth and a gay rag hearthrug up to the huge kitchen range. The scullery and larder stone floors were bare except for a border of chalk about a foot wide all the way round, which was renewed every week, applied with a wet cloth when the stones were washed.

The kitchen was my favourite room, for it was cheerful and light with a large window looking on to the garden. The walls were decorated with pictures which in those days the grocers and other tradespeople would give to their customers at Christmas. They were not framed, but hung from a black wooden roller which was repeated at the bottom to keep the picture from curling up. These were generally brightly coloured, rather crude reproductions of popular paintings such as Millais's 'Bubbles' and 'Cherry Ripe' or romantic scenes of sea or mountains.

In the middle of the room was the table, a large heavy one scrubbed perfectly white with the sand of which we had so much about us; and round the walls stood wooden chairs scrubbed to a like whiteness. In the afternoon this table was covered with a blue and red check cloth and all was cosy. The huge open range with the fire piled up and great hobs on each side with the ovens beneath, gleamed and shone.

This range was Fanny's special pride. The hobs on each side of the fire were black, polished with black lead, but the oven doors on each side of the fire were lavishly ornamented

22

with steel bands and knobs which Fanny kept polished like silver. It was one of my childish delights to go into the kitchen after our midday meal to see Fanny on her hands and knees, with a coarse sacking apron over her white one, polishing the stove with black lead, and the steel with fine ash from the fire, which she moistened with spit. The oven doors were steel; the large kitchen fender consisted of ornamental bands of steel, the centre being a heart-shaped plaque; and for more ornamentation, there was a large steel stool which stood shining before the fender in front of the fire. The whole effect was magnificent. Before putting the fender and the stool back in their places, Fanny would whiten the hearth which she first wetted with a cloth and then rubbed with a large piece of chalk; then she would smooth it with the damp cloth backwards and forwards until it presented an un-blemished area of gleaming whiteness, as the wet grey chalk dried quickly in the heat of the open fire. I used to long to take part in these activities and sometimes, if I was good and Fanny in a good humour, she would let me put the final polish to the steel fire-irons and I would do my best to imitate her.

Annie, during this time, had washed up at the stone sink in the scullery and the plates and dishes were put in piles on shelves on one side of the larder, the silver polished and put in its green baize-lined drawer and the steel knives cleaned by rubbing them on an emery-covered knife board. Annie had changed her dress for dinner into plain black with a pretty frilly apron and gophered cap with two streamers at the back. Fanny was still in her print dress; but having completed the range the kitchen then took on the appearance of a sitting-room all exquisitely neat and shining, the checked cloth on the table and the bright rag hearth-rug in front of the fire. Then Fanny would go upstairs and change into her black dress and pretty apron, for the worst of her day's work was over, as Annie got the tea ready, and supper which was a simple meal, ended Fanny's day's work.

In the evenings the maids would sit on the hard kitchen chairs at the table, either sewing or using their leisure as they liked. Once a week Mother would spend the afternoon with her maids in the kitchen, reading aloud to them while they sewed

—not 'improving' books but works of high literary quality such as the novels of George Eliot or Dickens or Baring Gould. Mother read aloud extremely well and we children were also allowed in the kitchen on these occasions to sit and listen. My sister Mary and I sat on low stools sewing dolls' clothes which Mother taught us to do properly. Hemming, running-and-felling, gathering, stroking the gathers and button-holing —we learned to do them quite young and I remember how when I hemmed my white calico for a doll's petticoat I would prick my finger and a line of little red dots appeared along the hem.

My mother regarded these two girls as in her charge and before their young men were allowed to visit them, which they did once a month, she interviewed them to see if she thought they were proper companions. Each maid had alter-native Sunday afternoons off duty to go out with her young man or to visit her family. Fanny was walking out and ex-pecting in the future to be married and she incurred my mother's great displeasure by allowing an itinerant salesman to persuade her to buy a sewing-machine for her bottom drawer in weekly payments. This of course was long before buying on the instalment system was common practice. My mother had a horror of debt and also of inferior goods sold at the door, and when Fanny confessed that she had paid the first instalment on a sewing machine of unknown make and to a travelling salesman, Mother was very angry. So much so that when the man came round for his second payment she made the poor trembling Fanny stay in the kitchen while she herself went to the back door to interview the wretch and to such effect that he meekly returned the money Fanny had paid him and the contract was cancelled. Mother then bought Fanny a reliable sewing-machine and Fanny paid her back month by month.

Mother's fear of debt reminds me how she told us children that when she was first married to Papa he, in frivolous mood, put a shilling each way on a horse. Mother prayed hard that it would lose, which it did, and that was the end of possible flutters in the future, and eventual ruin.

Annie's young man was a great favourite of mine. He worked in the glass factory at St Helen's and only came about

24

once a month to see Annie and he always brought something for me. Once it was a rat made of clear glass whose tail curved over his back: the joke was to fill him with water and blow down his snout, when the water rushed through the tail into your face. I was very much taken aback when this was first practised on me, by the laughter it caused. He also brought strange little twists of very fine brittle glass which you snapped in the middle so that they shattered into a thousand fragments. They made a sweet tinkling sound as they broke and we found them enchanting. Sometimes he brought a heavy sea-green glass paper-weight with a frosty fern imprisoned inside.

Fanny's young man worked at the Beecham Pill factory and he brought equally fascinating things to delight us children. These were squares of thin and apparently blank paper with a little black dot in one corner. On this dot one pressed a glowing match and immediately and mysteriously a pattern was traced out by the smouldering paper: sometimes it was a picture of animals or ships in full sail, sometimes just a few words of praise for the pills. Such things never failed to astonish us.

On special occasions my father would take Mother's place in the kitchen for the reading aloud and this the maids loved, for the Master was genial and kind and never found fault with them. He would read perhaps Wilkie Collins's *The Woman in White* or *The Moonstone*, or sometimes a poem or two by Tennyson or Wordsworth.

Everything in that house was harmonious, my mother very much at the head of affairs: a wonderful manager. But it is difficult to believe that in those days a leg of mutton could be bought for half-a-crown, whiskey at three shillings and six-pence a bottle, and oysters for a shilling a dozen.

SUNDAY

OF ALL THE Sundays in the year Whit Sunday was the only one which offered any deviation from the ordinary custom. On that day, whatever the weather—and in Lancashire where we lived it was often very cold still—we suddenly changed from winter clothes to summer ones. We discarded our flannel underclothes—how glad we were to be rid of the red flannel petticoat deemed necessary for protection against winter chills—and put on calico chemises, emitting protesting but pleased cries when the cold material touched our skin. The change from winter to summer garments proceeded through all the layers, and there were many in those days—chemise, bodice, starched petticoat edged with *broderie anglaise*, frilly drawers—until our dresses were reached. These were made of pretty light woollen material, often with short jackets to match, which Mother had most beautifully embroidered. Hats, too, generally of straw, with ribbon streamers, completed our new outfit, and we sat waiting for Mama and Papa to begin the long walk to the Church where we had our own pew and our own especially high hassocks. Mary and I walked side by side, our starched underclothes rustling. 'Have you both got handkerchiefs and your penny for the collection?' Mama would ask, and having received assurance on these important points, little if any conversation passed between us two girls and our parents.

We enjoyed Sunday. Wearing our best clothes was exciting and if the hymns were familiar, the singing among many people was exciting too. Sometimes my father, who was a friend of the parson and who had intended to be a clergyman himself, read the lesson, and then what reflected glory we felt and how our young friends envied us!

The long walk home along the streets dusted with sand blown from the sandhills nearby was a bit of an anti-climax, but the hot dinner of saddle of mutton and red-currant jelly, boiled and roast potatoes, greens and parsnips or carrots, followed by apple tart which Fanny had prepared for us, made up for our tiredness, and when Mother said, 'I think, James, that our children look as well as any', and Father smiled on us, we were two happy children.

In winter and summer we had two dresses for each season —a day dress and a good dress for Sundays and visiting. The following year the good dress became the day dress and a new good dress superseded the last year's one. Dresses were always lined and everything, underclothes and all, boots and gaiters in winter, were fastened with quantities of buttons. 'Please do me up, Nellie,' Mary would say, presenting her back to have the buttons fastened which she could not reach. Boot buttons were fastened with a magical twist of a button-hook, a difficult knack, fascinating once it had been mastered.

*   *   *

Nellie Noble's childhood was affected by illness. In later life she realized that her intense self-consciousness easily turning to shame and tears of humiliation was probably caused by the fact that she had seldom felt entirely well. Esther Noble, whose first duty was towards her invalid husband so that he could do his literary work, seems often to have been harsh towards the middle daughter.

*James reviewed books and regularly contributed to a number of literary journals—*The Daily Chronicle, Westminster Gazette, The Spectator, The Athenaeum, The Yellow Book *are some of them—but* The Manchester Examiner *was the family's chief source of income, sending each month a great hamper filled with books—fiction, biography, belles lettres, children's books—from which James could select what he wanted to review, and to which the children had access. Most of the novels were in three volumes then—Nellie remembered reading Hardy's* A Pair of Blue Eyes *from this source. When James and Esther and the children had read all they wanted, the books were sent to the 'Pinner Man' who bought review copies and it was upon the Pinner Man's cheque the family depended for a tidy sum each month as a substantial addition to their family income.*

Nellie then was sickly, catching any illness that was prevalent and having it badly. Mary was pretty, clever, obedient and happy, Irene headstrong, domineering and wilful. There was a typhoid epidemic in Liverpool and Nellie developed the disease. Her mother told her afterwards how certain streets were cordoned off with black flags hung to warn tradesmen not to go near. Soon after recovering from this fever, Nellie developed a tubercular gland in her neck which was cut and drained through a tube that had to be renewed at regular intervals. She remembered going alone to the doctor's surgery to have this painful business done and how sick and faint she felt afterwards, struggling home holding on to the iron railings.

But there were other memories of her mother which she enjoyed recalling. One day a number of crippled boys from an orphanage were brought to Southport for an outing. They came in a large horse-drawn wagonette and were lifted out and set down on the pavement by the attendants, looking out to sea, their backs against a wall, little white-faced boys, pale and sweating, with twisted legs or club-feet or what was then called hip-disease. The attendants went off to enjoy themselves, while the sun poured down on the boys in their black serge suits and starched collars. Esther Noble, with Mary and Nellie hand in hand passed by the still, quiet row. Briskly she retraced her steps to the greengrocer's and bought two large melons. She took these home, sliced them up and spread the slices on a napkin, taking them to the boys on a tray and offering each one a slice. But not one of the boys would take it—they had never seen or tasted melon before and were suspicious of it. Mrs Noble had to return home with the fruit untasted.

That story reminded Helen of a similar incident, but in reverse. One of their friends was giving a large children's party one Christmas and hired a small church hall for the purpose. All the mothers were to bring a contribution to the feast. Mrs Noble's great friend had made several blancmanges for the party and had used a new green colouring matter, rather too freely, so that these quivering edifices were a vivid moss-colour. Mrs Noble had had a preview of these delicacies, and when Nellie and Mary were being dressed for the party, she told them that on no account were they to eat any of these green blancmanges as they were poisonous. Even if their great friend whom they called 'Aunt' offered them some, they were to refuse at all costs. Fortunately in those

28

days children did what they were told submissively without saying, as they would not hesitate to do nowadays, 'Mother says we are not to have any of your green blancmange as it would poison us.'

Another time, posters appeared in the town depicting a fairy-like creature in diaphanous dress seated on the palm of a showman's hand, the showman in silk hat and top boots. Helen gazed in rapture at these posters and begged Mama to take her to see the midget, Madame Babette. Mama refused, guessing what the reality would be and disliking vulgar displays. Helen then went to Papa to plead, and after some spirited words from Mama, he promised to take her if she was very good. The show took place in a small hall and because Helen was short-sighted, Papa and she sat in the front. By and by, after the usual showman's patter about Madame Babette's having been presented to all the crowned heads of Europe, he vanished into the wings and returned with a little painted wizened and frizzed creature sitting on his shoulder, her long head and foreshortened stubby arms and legs bedizened with feathers and lace and sequins. The showman walked slowly by the front row, with the dwarf ogling and raising the frills of her skirt, blowing kisses and waving and offering to kiss all the children in the audience. Helen screamed with terror and bursting into loud sobs hid her face in Papa's lap, hysterically crying, 'No no, take me out, take me home.' Which Papa kindly did. Mama's greeting on their return was tight-lipped.

But Helen's first play was a different matter. That was the beginning of a lifelong devotion to the theatre. When the family returned to London, the three Noble sisters waited hours in pit queues to see the first nights of plays with Mrs Patrick Campbell, Beerbohm Tree, Forbes-Robertson and Henry Irving. While they were waiting to see a performance of The Second Mrs Tanqueray, *George Alexander who played opposite Mrs Patrick Campbell noticed the three girls as he went in at the stage-door, nodded to them, and later sent them out a tray of tea and cakes by the stage-door keeper, with his compliments. The headstrong Irene, a devotee of Sarah Bernhardt's, actually got to know her and was invited to one of her house-parties at Belle Isle.*

*   *   *

NELLIE'S FIRST PLAY

I WAS ABOUT ten and my younger sister Mary was seven years old. We were still known as 'the children' to distinguish us from our elder sister Irene, who dwelt in the realms of cleverness and scholastic successes far above our infantile reach, and who was regarded by us with awe and a good deal of fear. And from our brother Lancelot, who was very much younger, and being the only boy, was spoilt and indulged in a way which filled our young hearts with envy. Excitement and treats seldom came the way of 'the children', whose placid happy days were spent among their dolls and being taken for walks on the sandhills, or best of all being read aloud to by Father, who from an early age instilled in us an enthusiasm for Dickens. It never occurred to us to envy Irene when, for instance, she went to a fancy dress ball, in a midnight blue satin dress spangled with silvery stars arranged in their constellations and with a large glittering crescent on her head, or to feel aggrieved that Mary and I shared a rather bare attic as a bedroom, while Irene's room on the first floor had a real dressing-table with a looking-glass and a Liberty colour scheme of brown and gold, for which Mother had embroidered the curtains and bedspreads in marigolds; these we regarded as her right, just as she did. Her world and ours hardly touched, for though she went as a boarder to the school we attended as day children, our life in the elementary school—as it was called—in the basement, and hers with the brilliant, specially chosen 'Study' girls who composed sonnets and won gold bracelets as prizes, were as far removed from each other's as a mole's life is from a lark's.

So it was an altogether surprising and hardly believable event when Irene burst into Father's study, which was also the family's sitting-room, and exclaimed, 'Mama, you simply must take the children to see Minnie Palmer in *My Sweetheart* which is being played at the Southport Theatre. Miss Simon has taken the study-girls to see it and it is a most lovely play.'

We children, sitting on stools by our mother who was supervising our sewing, could not believe our ears. We had heard of theatres, for our parents loved the play and sometimes went to Liverpool to see Henry Irving acting in *Hamlet* or *Nance Oldfield*, but we had never been to one, nor had we any idea what acting was. The possibility so suddenly offered us was deliciously exciting. 'Oh Mama! Please let us go, oh please Papa, say we may go!' For our mother had often to be persuaded by Father.

And so it was that on the following afternoon we were dressed in our best frocks, red woollen dresses beautifully smocked and worn with wide silk sashes tied in a big bow behind. We wore our bronze kid dancing sandals, held on by fine elastic crossed at our ankles, on our black-stockinged feet. We were to go in 'Andrews's', the cab which, driven by Andrews, took us to school on wet days. He was as delighted as we were that we were to have such a treat, for he had known us since our babyhood and admired Father as a very learned gentleman and a writer of books.

The drive from Birkdale to Southport took some time, but Mary and I sat with our backs to the horses, speechless and pale with excitement, while Mama and Irene sitting opposite chatted as though nothing extraordinary were happening.

The theatre in Southport was a small but elegant Victorian building: a bit flamboyant in its decorations and in its gilded and encrimsoned gaslit interior, but to us it was a palace of beauty and splendour.

We sat in a row very near the stage, Mama at one end, Irene at the other and we two bemused children between them staring at the drop-scene which hid the stage. The orchestra had not yet filed into their pit, so the drop-scene occupied all our attention. It represented a scene in the grounds of Windsor Castle, with ladies in crinolines and top-hatted gentlemen on glossy horseback and children playing with hoops and puppies. There were fountains and beds of bright flowers; fine trees under whose shade chairs and tables stood, and richly dressed people sat at them, or reclined on the grass. A river flowed in the distance and upon it floated boats in which ladies with parasols sat, while swans preened in the rushes by the bank. We had never set eyes on anything so wonderful; I thought that this was what we had come to see, and I was perfectly content that it should be so. That there should be anything behind that magic picture never

31

dawned on me.

What then was our surprise when, first of all, the orchestra trooped in and began tuning their instruments, and then the conductor bowed to the audience and rapped on his rostrum and Mama and Irene propelled two bewildered little girls to their feet while 'God Save the Queen' was played. The drop-scene rolled up and displayed before our eyes a scene which enchanted us to a degree impossible to describe. We looked upon a real garden with hollyhocks and geraniums growing in it, with real green grass and a real arbour entwined with honeysuckle and roses, in which sat a lady, the most exquisite creature that we had ever seen. She wore a large hat trimmed with roses over her curls, and a pink muslin dress all flounces and ribbons. She strolled out of the arbour on the arm of a young man to whom she talked, while a real little pomeranian dog yapped at her heels. In the centre of the garden hung a swing and in its seat the ravishing lady sat while the gentle-man swung her to and fro, her frills and ribbons billowing and frothing, and both sang a song which far surpassed in romance and melody anything that I had imagined from the fairy stories Mama had read to us.

The scene changed and we were now in a room with a French window opening on to this very garden—I recognized the hollyhocks and a corner of the arbour—through which more people came, including a neat and dainty little parlour-maid in a full-skirted rustling black dress under which, as she moved with her tray of silver tea-things, we could see frilly lace petticoats and trim ankles in black silk stockings. And to make all perfect she wore the daintiest muslin apron and little cap to match with floating ribbons. She was the exact replica of a tiny doll I had been given for my dolls' house, and the idea that my doll had come to life was not more miraculous than all else. She was pert and saucy and when the young man who had swung the lady kissed her, I remember looking up to my mother's face to show my de-light to her, and was abashed to see serious disapproval in her expression.

The room itself was to my mind the most elegant and beautiful apartment I could have imagined. All glittering with mirrors draped with gorgeous silk hangings and curtains with long fringes and tassels, lots of small tables and little gilded chairs and stools, and in every corner pots of ferns and palms. A real mantelpiece was ornamented with candlesticks standing in the midst of hanging glass prisms, and a great gilded clock in the centre, supported by plump gold cherubs. Birds in fanciful cages hung at the windows. It was everything that contrasted with our own sitting-room at home, which being also Father's study was lined with books, with his writing table in the bay window. The sofa on which he often lay had a plain rug over the leather, and the easy chairs were covered with dark green velvet.

This rich room, all sparkle and colour, seemed to me the ideal place for these enchanted beings to live, and in it and the garden I believed they *did* live, beings of another sphere, whose lives were all singing and dancing and play, colour and laughter. I cannot remember the plot of this innocent little comedy, with its Victorian pretty-pretty romance and its childish make-believe; but to me it was a vision of real life on which for a little while I had been privileged to gaze.

When the final curtain came down and the now sadly begrudged drop scene hid the stage, I did not understand that the gaiety, happiness and romance had come to an end. That the dresses were packed into hampers and the golden curls unpinned, and that the green grass was rolled up or that the pomeranian had any other home. For a space I had been permitted to see another unsuspected and unsuspecting world and I firmly believed that it went on behind the mute drop scene for ever and ever.

Minnie Palmer is for me one of the immortals.

WINTERSDORF SCHOOL

THE SCHOOL my parents chose for us was unique, before the standardization which makes very little difference between one school and another. This school was run by an old lady and her two middle-aged daughters: Miss Mary Simon was the head of the teaching staff, and Miss Sarah looked after the domestic arrangements. It occupied a large house, long and low, in another part of the suburb of Southport in which we lived. It was a boarding school, called 'Wintersdorf', but a few day girls were allowed to attend, and the Misses Simon, being intimate friends of my parents, I think allowed us to come without fees.

My eldest sister, Irene, decided that she wanted to be a boarder. She was determined and strong-willed and generally had what she wanted, as in this case. But Mary and I, aged about seven and ten, went as day girls.

The school was some two miles from our house, which was a good trudge for children, but in those days the hard way was not considered unsuitable. We were brought up in what would now be considered spartan harshness, but it was not really so bad and we were happy. We stayed all day at school and my elder sister carefully rehearsed to us the way we should behave at table. We must on no account blow on our pudding, or take up a chicken bone in our fingers, and at teatime a curious custom was observed, which we thought very lavish—we could help ourselves to great gobbets of jam out of the beautiful crystal dishes. The jam was then to be eaten with a fork. These refinements made me particularly nervous.

The house stood in extensive park-like grounds and was a fine dignified building of the late eighteenth century, a country-house type of dwelling. When you went in at the front door you were in a spacious hall like a huge room, from the end of which rose a magnificent staircase of wide, shallow stairs which at the top branched out right and left on to a landing as big as the hall below. But these stairs were not used by the smaller children. We were housed and had our lessons in the basement, and a staircase of a very different kind led down to our dungeon-like classrooms. If we wanted to go to the first floor we used the servants' back stairs. In this basement were also the music-rooms—little glass boxes with a piano in each—about six or eight of them. Our classroom—there was only one—was large with small windows whose lower halves were flush with the ground, and whose top halves looked out on to the garden. Desks with lids were ranged in rows and there were about twenty children in the class, girls of eight to eleven years old.

A numerous staff of women taught us and Miss Sarah was deputed to do some teaching of the little children. Outside the classroom was a dark sort of ante-room where we hung our coats and hats and changed from our walking shoes into slippers.

Wintersdorf existed for the daughters of rich north country manufacturers and professional people; they came from Lancashire, Yorkshire and even Northumberland and were for the most part from homes of cultured people; but there was also a slight admixture of the vulgar rich at whom Miss Mary looked very askance.

When we started school my elder sister Irene had been there for some time and had done brilliantly. Each year a prize of a gold bracelet was offered for the best sonnet written by a girl in the upper forms and Irene twice won this prize. The poems were sent to William Watson who judged them. The sonnets had no name attached so he was quite unaware that a daughter of a great friend of his, James Ashcroft Noble, had entered the competition. I remember one sonnet which she wrote had for its subject a picture by Frank Dicksee called 'Is it nothing to you all ye that pass by?' which depicted a romantic pair of young lovers in mediaeval dress laughing together as they walked hand in hand down a street in Italy. Crouching by the wall of a house was a beggar holding up a crucifix to the young couple, who took no notice of it. Irene shone in other ways, too, writing stories and plays—for this school put the arts before everything, and we acted and played and sang and danced and wrote poetry much more than formal exercises in arithmetic and geography. But I am speaking now of activities shared by the older girls.

In the elementary school, as it was called, the little children had interesting lessons in which essay writing took a

35

prominent part. We each had our own desk with a lid which was our private property, and we ornamented the insides of these lids with Christmas cards fixed on with drawing pins, or pretty pieces of seaweed or shells stuck on with gum, or anything that we thought pretty and precious. All the little girls vied with each other on the insides of their desk lids.

My sister Irene was, as I have said, brilliant in everything that she did; so was my younger sister, Mary, whose sweet docile nature and pretty fair curling hair won all hearts. She was also self-confident and independent and was a great success at the elementary school.

When we first went to Wintersdorf together Miss Mary said to me, 'Now Helen, are you too going to be a bright and shining light of the elementary school?' and I remained dumb and awed and despondent, for I knew I should not be so. I was a plain child, with dark straight hair cut like a boy's, which was the fashion, with a thick fringe, and I wore spectacles. Nobody in those days wore bright colours and until a little later period than I write of we wore plain brown frocks, rather long, and black woollen stockings.

The classes I remember best were History, with tales of the *Morte d'Arthur* and the Kings and Queens of England, the Princes in the Tower, the castles and palaces, which fired my imagination. But what I loved best was when one of our teachers in perhaps the Geography class told us of other countries or English country where there were fields and flowers and trees which I had read of in fairy tales but had never seen. I remember Miss Sarah was taking the class one day and was talking about the relative merits of forests and open fields. Now forests, when I read about them in stories, were mysterious and fascinating places to me and I longed to see a forest—I had no idea what it was like. Miss Sarah said, 'Now if you were going to have a picnic, Helen, where would you choose to have it—in the open field full of flowers, where the sun would shine and the ground would be dry for sitting on the grass and where you could run about and play with your ball or skip; or in the forest, where great trees cast a dark shade and where few flowers grew and where moss and fungus and undergrowth were always damp from the dripping of the trees?' And I said, 'I would rather go to the forest, Miss

36

Sarah.' 'Oh, Helen, what a silly child you are,' she replied. And that was the end of that. But I thought in my heart, 'I will go into the forest', but I did not dare of course to say a word. So it was always—I never gave the right answer and plunged deeper and deeper into self-conscious failure, while my little sister rose higher and higher in the school's approval. She was soon moved into the upper school and I was left below.

I remember once the subject for an essay was 'A Trip Round the Coast of England in a Ship'. I had never been in a ship, though of course I had seen the sea by which I lived, so the subject seemed hopeless, for I had no experience from which to recount. I believe I had in fact been taken on holiday to the Isle of Man, but was so ill with seasickness all the way over that I had no recollection of it. However, I loved writing because I could do it in solitude and preferred it to being questioned. So I wrote away, and my fellows looked with amazement as I filled page after page of my exercise book. The essays were sent in and to my astonishment and bewilderment, because I thought there had been a mistake, my name appeared at the top of the list and I had full marks for my essay!

But this success did not raise me in my own estimation even when my companions said, 'Fancy Nellie getting full marks!' which I knew was a most rare occurrence.

At this time—though as a little child I was quite unaware of it—the 'greenery yallery Grosvenor Gallery' fashion set in and Liberty's in London exploited the beautiful colours and materials which came from the East—greens, blues, ambers and pinks, and the school under Miss Simon whole-heartedly adopted this craze and so did my parents. Our dresses, from being ugly and dull, were now made of beautiful soft woollen material exquisitely smocked or embroidered, and most of the girls, little and well-grown, who came from the cultured homes of Liverpool, Manchester and York, adopted this fashion. The older girls dressed in graceful and loose dresses with sashes of silk round their waists and big bows behind. Japanese fans and Japanese china decorated their dormitories, and gauzy scarves with rainbow colours were draped over their looking-glasses or the heads of their beds.

My father used to come and lecture to the older girls once a week about poetry and literature in general. The pre-Raphaelites were well to the fore. We learned the poems of Christina Rossetti and of Rossetti himself, some of Swinburne and of course Tennyson. At that time his *Idylls of the King* and his other poems were extremely popular; many girls were named Maude and many boys Lancelot.

The prizes given for artistic or intellectual attainments were of surprising beauty and value. There were twelve picked pupils of Miss Mary's who inhabited a special room and were called the 'study girls'. These were chosen by Miss Mary partly for their characters as gentlewomen, partly for their artistic achievements. They all wore beautiful dresses and their classroom, which was more like a parlour, was full of lovely things. The prizes consisted often of delicate miniature reproductions of famous pieces of sculpture or plaques framed and glazed, perhaps four in a frame, repeating in miniature scenes from the Parthenon frieze. Art books also and pictures by Burne-Jones, Holman Hunt and other famous artists were given as rewards. Literature was one of the chief subjects taught in the school, and my love of Shakespeare began at Wintersdorf. We acted his plays in class, each taking a part, and I could at one time recite by heart almost the whole of *The Merchant of Venice*, *A Midsummer Night's Dream*, *Twelfth Night* and *The Tempest*. I acted in these plays; but to be asked—as I often was—to take part in these dramatic recitals was terrible for me, as I was shy and diffident. However, secretly I loved the poetry and the stories of the plays and later, when we did historical plays, *Julius Caesar* and *Henry V*, I learned most of my history in that way. But I only took part because I was in the class and everyone had to, and I was terrified of appearing before the staff in the character I had been given.

We learned poetry also, Wordsworth and Tennyson particularly, and lines like 'Oh the difference to me' in the poem 'She dwelt beside untrodden ways', and 'Break, break, break, on thy cold grey stones' filled me with a strange and uplifting emotion which I did not understand. 'Tears, idle tears' used to affect me in the same way and other lines set my romantic imagination on fire as a child.

But school was hateful to me, for I was lost among a lot of gay self-confident girls, pretty and popular, and I wept many tears of humiliation.

Sometimes Miss Mary would gather a class in the spacious hall and teach us how to behave socially. She would tell us when we entered a room to walk right in and not sit on the seat nearest the door, and if our hostess were there, to greet her before we spoke to anyone else. She showed us how to manipulate a tea-cup in our hand with a sandwich or cake in the saucer, and how to thank our hostess after a party was over. And how to step into and down from a carriage gracefully, without displaying our ankles. We also learned how to walk in the street: Miss Simon stood at one end of the hall and the girls one by one had to walk towards her. I remember this dreadful ordeal because Miss Mary said, 'Helen, you waddle!' which none of the other girls did. We were taught how to greet a passing acquaintance in the street when we saw her at some distance away. We were shown how to begin to incline our heads so that at the moment we passed her the bow was perfected, and the smile accompanying this acknowledgement was begun at the same time as the inclination and came to the climax when we passed. All this I found extremely difficult, but I have remembered these lessons to this day and think them very sensible, to make gauche girls behave in a dignified and frank manner.

Grace and beauty in movement and speech were part of the education, and we practised what were called calisthenics. We learned graceful movements of arms and hands, often with fans and sometimes with the gauzy scarves I have mentioned. We did this to classical music, Chopin very often, and Mendelssohn, and we wore dresses of carefully chosen colour schemes. The whole school took part in these exercises and I think, looking back, it must have been beautiful to watch. Sometimes Miss Simon hired a hall and we did the whole thing in public to an invited audience. This was a great annual event in Southport—Miss Simon's Wintersdorf Girls' Calisthenics. Sometimes it was not so pretty, when we used Swedish clubs and dumb-bells and marching—but always fine music accompanied these exercises and I enjoyed it very much.

Our behaviour at table, too, was supervised and we learned

to look after our neighbour. We were not allowed to ask for the potatoes or the jam to be passed to us, but must wait, sometimes rather anxiously, to be offered the dish. I remember one of the teachers at the midday meal watching me arrange my plum stones on the edge of my plate, preparatory to discovering if I should marry a soldier or a sailor, saying to me, 'Miss Nellie, kindly descend your stones!'

When eventually I reached the upper school, sometimes the girls were invited into Miss Simon's drawing room, a room decorated in soft colours, beautiful pictures and rich hangings; the upholstered chairs and sofas were covered with amber velvet, and cushions to contrast with this colour—soft browns and subtle shades of green—littered the sofas. The carpets were plain felt, with Persian rugs over them, and on the mantelpiece of the fireplaces—of which the drawing room had two—were delicate Venetian glass ornaments and vases and statuettes. In the fireplaces the fires were small and to my mind extremely elegant, and I thought how vulgar our great blazing fires were at home, with their heaped up coals and flames half way up the chimney.

At this time I had a great desire to learn to play the violin, and when I pressed my parents to allow me to do this, they consulted Miss Simon, with the result that a violin was bought for me and a girl of about fifteen, who was proficient with the instrument—Adeline Greaves, a very pre-Raphaelite looking girl with abundant hair and a beautiful profile—was deputed to teach me. She thought little of me as a pupil and these lessons were soon discontinued. I then became the pupil of the violin master, Mr Minchin, who came once a week to the school. These violin lessons were held in the smaller of the two drawing rooms which opened out of each other with folding doors, and Mr Minchin, an elderly man whom I liked very much, was pleased with my progress. When I could play Handel's 'Largo' my parents were delighted.

I remember well the dresses then in fashion, with bustles, of some of the young women staff. There were two kinds of bustle, one where the skirt was drawn up at the back into a sort of bunch of material, and the other which was called a 'waterfall' bustle. This latter I thought not so pretty, but more elegant. The bustle consisted of a sort of shelf springing out from the small of the back about six inches, supported underneath in some way. The dress was made of green velvet. Masses of material hung from this shelf in full folds, and the name 'waterfall' gave a descriptive idea of its design. Of course all dresses swept the ground, except children's, and there was much grace and dignity in the women's clothes.

We had prayers every morning, the whole school together in the Hall, and the hymn that my father had written was sung to a tune composed by one of the staff. The piano was played by one of the girls in turn. Concerts were given regularly, piano recitals and singing and the recitation of poetry.

Famous people came to lecture at the school. William Watson came and gave us a recital of music—he was a wonderful pianist—and Richard le Gallienne, a protégé of Father's, came to speak on the subject of 'Beauty', and once Oscar Wilde visited the school to lecture to us on 'The Home Beautiful'. He was a rising star then in the world of art and literature, and my father admired him very much. (Later, Father was one of the many sympathizers who signed a petition against the harshness of Oscar Wilde's prison sentence.) So it can be seen that it was an unusual school, and I for one —though I was not happy there—benefited from its influence.

No games entered into our curriculum, but we were taken for walks on the sandhills and found the exquisite Grass of Parnassus in what were called the Slacks—the hollows filled with water in the winter where this flower grew—and also Wintergreen and other uncommon flowers which I have since found in Scotland.

The sandhills were covered with tufts of what we called star-grass, a sort of reedy spikey grass which prevented the sand from blowing about, though drifts of it escaped into the streets. We played ball and other games there and I loved these outings.

While I was at Wintersdorf the first that I recall of a number of terrible epidemics of influenza occurred; people died in the streets, and the number of deaths was frightening. It attacked the school and several girls died. The funeral of one took place at the school, and was conducted with the characteristic touch of artistry and drama. The girls closely connected with the dead were dressed in white and the coffin was white; the flowers were not made up into wreaths or crosses, but were strewn, Ophelia-wise, in exotic profusion over the coffin. The whole school attended the funeral. Those dressed in white were privileged study girls. I cannot now imagine how the parents of the dead girl accepted all this, but so it was: and I remember a hymn of my father's composition being sung as the coffin was being taken from the school hall down to the church. Here my memory fails, but this scene impressed itself vividly on my childish mind.

But after some years of the closest intimacy between the Misses Simon and my parents, who even spent the summer holidays together in various furnished houses in Wales, it all came to an end. I do not know all the details, but it was concerned with a lecture my father was to give in Southport, which Miss Simon would not attend with her girls because of an epidemic, I think; but whatever the reason, it meant some financial loss to Father, and great bitterness and misunderstanding resulted between our parents and the Misses Simon. We left Southport to go to Liverpool, and ultimately to London.

Our house, to the end of my father's life, contained many lovely things which Miss Simon had given him: mahogany bookcases, a silver inkstand and an ivory-handled walking-stick are some of the things I remember. Also a charming watercolour full-length painting of Father commissioned by Miss Simon from a young artist, whose name curiously enough was Edward Thomas. This I have now and it depicts my father sitting in a sort of green velvet deck-chair, the woodwork of which is carved to simulate bamboo, and whose cushion is lavishly fringed; on a table by his side is a beautiful glass vase with a single purple iris in it, typical of the new fashion in decoration which Winterdorf had adopted so whole-heartedly.

*   *   *

The family, now fairly prosperous, moved back to the Wandsworth Common district of London, into a more spacious house with a large garden at the back where a great cherry tree dominated the lawn. Nellie found it difficult to understand the southerners' speech and intonation—she still spoke with a strong Lancashire accent, using the short 'a'. The Londoners' unfriendliness and inhospitality, too, struck her at once. In the north, when a family moved house, neighbours would be round at once to give help and to bring trays of tea and bread and butter. In London no one paid any attention to the tired newcomers. As soon as they had moved in to 6 Patten Road, however, the tradesmen hoped for their custom: the baker left a miniature cottage loaf and a tiny iced cake, the grocer samples of his Indian and China teas and the dairy an earthenware jar of cream.

Irene had left home by now and Nellie, considered to be the domestic one as she did not shine intellectually, helped her mother get the new house in order, choosing curtain material, carpets and so on.

On one of these shopping expeditions in the West End Nellie noticed with great curiosity the painted and befeathered ladies waiting about around Piccadilly Circus and asked her mother who they were and what they were doing. 'They go to bed with men,' answered Mrs Noble sharply. 'Go to bed with men!' exclaimed Nellie incredulously, 'Whatever for?' 'All men are beasts, including your father,' was her mother's reply, which was all that she ever said to her daughter of the 'facts of life'.

This suggestion that her adored father could ever be considered a 'beast' was a cruel and bewildering shock to Helen, and I think from those blunt words of her mother's and their mysterious and horrifying implications which Helen could not possibly reconcile with the gentle, popular and generous-hearted man she loved above all others—from those words Helen's slight fear and deep respect for her mother changed to distrust, even dislike.

Mary and Helen attended one of the Girls' Public Day School Trust schools at Wimbledon, under an exceptional headmistress, while Lancelot went to the Merchant Taylors' School. Helen's love of literature was very much widened and encouraged by a beloved English teacher, Miss Fowler, who recognized her good qualities that at Wintersdorf had been outshone by the 'bright and shining lights' of Irene and Mary. But she still hated school and was considered dull by the *other teachers and begged to be allowed to leave when she was sixteen. Her mother who was glad of some extra help in the larger house, where she and James entertained a good deal though his health was not improving, allowed Helen to stay at home.*

The memories of this time, before she went as nursery governess to various families, is not vivid to Helen, though she remembers well the journey every Sunday to a fashionable chapel in Bloomsbury Square, frequented by intellectuals of the time, who came to hear a well-known Irishman, Stopford-Brooke, give a series of lectures, rather than sermons, on Tennyson. The Noble family walked to Clapham Junction where they took a train to Waterloo and then a horse bus in which, for a halfpenny put into a box below the driver's seat, they were driven across Waterloo Bridge and then walked the rest of the way to Bloomsbury Square. Helen remembered that during the service parties of tourists would come in and be shown around and famous people were pointed out—Mrs Humphrey Ward was one of them—with unhushed voices, and having absorbed this bit of culture, they would take a noisy leave.

It was at the Unitarian Chapel, nearer home, which the Noble family attended a year or so later, that Mr Tarrant, the minister, introduced Mr and Mrs Philip Henry Thomas and their six handsome sons, who also attended the chapel, to the Nobles.

*   *   *

Helen's first job when she left school was that of nursery governess. Monsieur and Madame Roman occupied a suite of rooms at the Hotel Metropole in Northumberland Avenue. He was a Russian aristocrat and his wife a beautiful and timid Austrian who had been trained as an opera singer. Their only child was a boy of five—'His name is Horst—as in Chiselhorst', Madame explained. Madame Roman was as gentle and submissive as her tall handsome husband was arrogant and, Helen feared, cruel. Helen came daily and looked after Horst, teaching him to read, playing chess with him and taking him for walks in the London parks and gardens, together with his

44

beloved and invisible playmate, Mabel. Usually Helen stayed until the evening meal, dining with the family and then putting Horst to bed. Sometimes, when the parents were out for the evening, a supper tray would be sent up for the child and Miss Noble, and when Horst had been put to bed and read a story, Helen would stay with some sewing or a book until they came back, when Monsieur would send her home in a hansom back to Wandsworth Common.

Each evening, when Horst was to dine with his parents in the hotel dining room, the man from Swears & Wells, then the most exclusive shop for children's clothes, would come to the nursery to dress the child in full Highland rig, lace cravat, velvet doublet, kilt, tartan stockings complete with skian dhu, silver-buckled shoes, in order that everything should be absolutely correct. Once downstairs at the dining table however the correctness vanished, as Horst was allowed to have anything he liked for dinner. His usual preference was for a tumblerful of strawberry jam.

On one occasion when Helen was dining with them Monsieur ordered roast chicken and all that went with it. When the bread sauce was served, it was an unattractive thin but lumpy grey-looking liquor and Monsieur asked the waiter angrily what it was supposed to be. Helen, nervous and hoping to prevent a scene, said that it was bread sauce, but that when her mother made it the result was creamy and fluffy, flavoured with cloves and onion. 'Do you know how to make it?' asked Monsieur sharply and when the nervous girl acquiesced, he ordered Helen, whom he accompanied, to go to the kitchens and show the chef how to make it, which in an agony of embarrassment she was forced to do.

Helen admired Madame's beautiful clothes. Laid out on her bed, when it was time to change for dinner, were exquisite satin stays made to match the gown she was wearing, violet, crimson and gold, with milanese silk stockings in the same gorgeous colours. Her throat and wrists sparkled with diamonds and her hair, of course, was elaborately dressed by her maid every evening.

Sometimes Monsieur Roman would be away several days and then Helen would stay with Madame, in a bed in Horst's room, and the two young women would chat comfortably and Madame would ask with longing about the country, the flowers, woods and birds. Her greatest treasure was a primrose in a pot which Helen had brought back with her from a country walk with Edward.

A duty which Helen did not enjoy during Monsieur's frequent and unpredictable absences was that of having to take a cab to an office in Holborn of which she had been given a key. On the glass door of the office, inside a great block, was engraved the name of an aluminium company. Her job was to unlock the outer door where, on the floor below the letterbox, would be a large pile of letters with stamps from all over the world on their corners. The inner office had a desk and a chair or two, dusty and uncared for. Helen would collect the letters, close and lock the door and return to the Metropole in the waiting cab. At the time this was rather an adventure, though the empty, still office was a little sinister; it was not until many years afterwards that it dawned on Helen that Monsieur Roman was perhaps a member of the royal Romanov family, exiled perhaps, and receiving information and enquiries—about what and from whom?—from all parts of the world.

One day Madame told Helen that they were all going away for some weeks, but would get in touch with her again when they returned to London. Madame had tears in her eyes as Helen helped her to pack her trunks. Then there was little Horst to comfort—for he was looking all around their suite of rooms for his playmate Mabel, and was distraught that she had hidden because she did not want to go away. A fierce word in Russian from his father sent him to his trunk where he sat pale and wide-eyed, Helen telling him she would find Mabel and take care of her. The primrose was eased into Madame's muff while Monsieur's back was turned.

And that was the last that Helen saw or heard of them.

*　　　　　*　　　　　*

46

WILLIAM MORRIS

WHEN I was eighteen I was a serious-minded young woman: intelligent enough, but I fear lacking in humour, although with a capacity which I have retained all my long life for hero worship of those I thought great, of getting to know as much about them as possible, which has brought me much interest and pleasure to this day. The time of which I write was about 1895.

My eldest sister Irene, I and about four other girls, among them Chris Knewstub, whose father had been a friend of Rossetti's, and her very beautiful sister Grace, who later married William Orpen the painter, formed a little circle with the grandiose title of 'The London Research Society'. The research was of a very ephemeral kind, for it consisted chiefly in going to see places where famous people had lived, or looking at anything that had belonged to them or was in any way connected with them. For instance, one of our researches was to the British Museum where we were allowed by the librarian to handle the manuscript of Blake's *Songs of Innocence*. Another time we visited Keats's house at Hampstead and saw some of his manuscripts and the mulberry tree under which he wrote 'Ode to a Nightingale'. On another occasion we visited a man living in a fashionable part of London to see his relics of Walt Whitman. He was a slight acquaintance of one of our members and it astonishes me now to think of the kindness of strangers in allowing this intrusion of half a dozen raw young women whose only excuse for asking such favours was their keen enthusiasm. He had a death mask of Whitman but what particularly struck me was a plaster cast of Walt Whitman's hand—the hand of a countryman and worker. Hands—particularly strong working hands—have always appealed to me, and it was the strong yet sensitive workmanlike hands of Edward Thomas which first attracted me to him.

Owing to Chris Knewstub's association with Rossetti and our own keen interest in the pre-Raphaelites, we decided to 'research' Rossetti. We had only a few hours on Saturday afternoons for these activities and though they gave us pleasure, they added nothing to scholarship, as may be imagined.

47

William Morris was at that time living at Kelmscott House in Chiswick, and because my father and mother had once stayed there with the George Macdonalds who had occupied it before William Morris, I was deputed to write to William Morris to ask him if we might come to see his Rossettis and to hear anything he cared to tell us about our great pre-Raphaelites.

William Morris very kindly gave us permission to come and see him, so five of us set out for Kelmscott House. We walked there from Wandsworth Common, for that was part of the adventure. We were all about the same age, all immature and gauche and all interested in the arts: myself particularly in literature, and my sister Irene in pictures.

We arrived on Chiswick Mall at about three in the afternoon to find the beautiful house surrounded by scaffolding and ladders and workmen in process of redecorating. We knocked at the door and were admitted I think by a man-servant and shown into a room which overlooked the garden, not the river. I was extremely interested in the house because my parents had often described it to me when the family of George Macdonald lived there in untidy but strictly moral bohemianism. The chief features of the room into which we were shown were an enormous round oak table scrubbed to whiteness and on the wall a large tapestry depicting, I think, a scene from *Morte d'Arthur*, designed by Burne Jones but the handiwork of Morris himself.

We stood silently waiting for the appearance of our host. Presently the door opened and there stood before us a grey-haired, short and thickset man dressed in a blue linen smock. This I remember, for I loved such things. It was of the traditional pattern with a yoke of close and elaborate smocking which was repeated at the wrists. The shoulder pieces were beautifully embroidered in white thread, and so was the collar. He had an impressive head covered with thick grey hair.

When he set eyes on the five serious girls, only one of whom had any pretensions to good looks, he stood for some seconds speechless and motionless with obvious embarrassment, rumpling his hair with his hand. Then I, who had written the letter and was felt to be the authoritative one, having this slight connection with Kelmscott House, stepped forward and introduced the London Research Society. I told him how my father and mother had stayed in the house with the George Macdonalds and did my best to warm the icy atmosphere of shyness. Gradually our host became responsive to our obvious enthusiasm and in a little while he could not do enough to please us.

He brought out his own original drawings and manuscripts and his exquisite edition of Chaucer and reached down from a shelf illuminated manuscripts of the Middle Ages, all carefully kept in stiff outer coverings. I shall never forget the moment when one of us—happily not myself—touched very delicately the beautiful gold ornamentation of one of the parchments and the anger which flared up for a moment in our host. Morris told us that the gold was of so delicate a nature that it must never be touched. Our horror at what one of us had in ignorance done and the humiliation at his anger, I can feel to this day. But it was over in a moment and we breathed once more, worshipping the man who had so graciously forgiven us and who brought more and more lovely things to show us.

Some of the parchments had had holes where the skin was thin and worn and these had been darned across and across by nuns with fine linen thread, with exquisite skill and neatness, incorporating tiny patterns. William Morris told us that from this darning of parchments ornamented with minute flowers and formal designs sprang the idea of lace-making by interweaving on a network of linen threads. Much else of interest he told us which I have forgotten, but the gentle fancies of the nuns darning being the origin of lace-making stayed in my memory.

He told us that he could not show us over the house, which he would like to have done, because it was in the hands of workmen and covered with dust-sheets; but he ran up and down stairs and in and out of rooms bringing us pictures by Rossetti and Burne Jones and books and manuscripts for us to see. He talked especially to the Knewstub girls whose father he had known, and was obviously anxious for us to forget his momentary displeasure. Grace Knewstub, I used to think, was so like the painting of Rossetti's—the head of a girl with a mass of fair hair, wearing an amber necklace with a pendant heart, called 'Jolie Coeur'—that I used to imagine Rossetti had used her as a model.

I think we were with William Morris about an hour, and then after his shaking each of us by the hand, we left, thrilled and awed by this momentous interview.

The fifth member of the Society who was with us that day, whose name escapes me, was a journalist and she kept a record of the Society's activities, but I do not know if she ever made any use of it. The little company of earnest young women had to separate to go their ways and earn their livings; and I had met Edward Thomas.

II / LETTERS FROM HELEN 1896-1917

LETTERS FROM HELEN 1896-1917

Janet Hooton, née *Aldis, to whom most of these letters are addressed, was a girlhood friend and confidante of Helen's. Janet and Helen remained friends all their lives. Edward and Janet's husband, Harry Hooton, also became close friends. There are also some letters to Edward and one to Eleanor Farjeon.*

*   *   *

TO JANET ALDIS

2 January 1896   6 Patten Road
                                             Wandsworth Common
Dear Pal,

May 1896 be the happiest year you have ever spent, may you succeed in all you do, and may the happy events foretold by the spirits arrive soon. When you next hold converse with the inhabitants of Borderland, you might ask them if any such event is in preparation for me. I already guess their short but decided answer. No! I send you a picture of myself. Do I ever look like that? Heaven forbid! Perhaps I will when I am a full blown old maid, delivering a lecture to an audience like myself, old maids of uncertain ages, on the advisability of remaining single. We had a very quiet, but *very* happy Christmas. I long to see you especially today because I feel rather dumpy, and you who would blow me up to the skies for thus feeling without the least cause, would do me good. I have begun a diary and I can relieve my feelings, by writing down exactly what I want to say to anybody who would be fool enough to listen.

Do you remember Janet?, when I saw you last I told you of a plan I had made regarding the boy who father is taking up, and who writes Nature sketches. I think it will succeed although it will take ages, for he is fearfully shy, and I am likewise afflicted. He wants a girl friend and I want a boy friend, and as I like him (or at least what I know of him) and I *think* he likes me, I think it would be good for both of us if we could be friends. I wonder if we shall. I can see you Janet as you read this, with a broad grin overspreading your face. And my grin is even wider than yours. Mary is going to be very gay, having had three invitations to dances already. I have had one invitation, a dance, to which it is very doubtful I shall go because it is to be given such a long way out of town, and the getting home late would be so difficult.

Please give my love to all your family. How very, *very* kind it was of Aunt Emily [Janet's mother] to send me such a lovely present. Please give her my love, and many wishes for a bright and happy New Year. Please give my love to all the family. I do want to see you all, and I will some day even if I have to sell my soul for the railway fare. Would that I had a bike! Give my love especially to Maggie. I wish I knew her better. I feel as if we two have a tiny bit in common, only don't tell her I said so. And last you, to whom I send this gift with heaps of love and New Year wishes.

Yours very affectionately   Helen

6 January 1896   6 Patten Road
                                 Wandsworth Common

My dearest Janet,

As you will see when you get this letter it is no go. I was so excited when I got your letter, for I was sure that they would let me go. But I asked Mother, and she said I was to ask Father, and Father said I could not afford it, and it would not be worth while for such a short time. For I said I would only go 'til Friday so that Mother need not be long without me. What he means by not 'worth while' I don't know. I would rather spend my money on seeing you now even if only for a few hours, than on anything else in the world. And so when I heard my verdict I was so bitterly disappointed that I retired to my room and wept many a briny tear. Are you ashamed of me? If you are small blame to you. They simply can have no idea how much I want to see you, or else they would have let me go. I don't know why it is myself, but I feel I must talk to you, and hear you talk or else I shall do something desperate. I talk to Mary, and when I am blazing away and think for once that she is being or trying to be sympathetic, she asks, 'What are you going to wear at Mrs Jones's dance?' So I keep my feelings and thoughts to myself, and I feel as if I cannot contain them any longer. Weeping is not strong enough for how I feel, so if there are any smudges on this letter you will know they are tears. How jolly of Aunt Emily to say she would like to have me, and how jolly of you to write me such nice letters.

I and the Thomas boy are very slowly making our way. He wrote and asked father if I might go out with him on one of his long walks. To my surprise he said I might. So I was in a great state of elation. But to my disappointment Edward never turned up for me. And when he came last night and was asked the reason, he said he had never dreamed I would be allowed to come. But he is going to take me someday this week to some lovely woods he knows. Last night I was in a furious rage because Edward asked me to go to his home this afternoon, and he would show me some flowers and nests he thought I would like to see. So I gladly assented. But that little plan was soon put a stop to, for mother would not let me go by myself, and there was nobody to go with me. Did you ever hear such awful tommy rot in your life? I call it very wrong. Mother says What would Mrs Thomas think? I say if she thought till she was tired, she could not possibly think of any wrong. I feel so cramped in. I want to expand my ideas and views, but how can I? When I appeal to Mary she says like a good obedient child 'Mother knows best' in which I do not agree with her. I know Mother has been brought up in the narrowest groove, and I have often wondered how it is that her ideas are so broad as they are. So now I have to wait until Lance [Helen's brother, six years younger than herself] can go with me, to play propriety I suppose . . . Here I am eighteen years old, and in a great state of elation because I am going out with a boy. It is disgusting and immoral and a disgrace. Why we may go walks together, and not go to his house where there is all his family I simply cannot imagine. It is too deep for me. When I have children I shall bring them up in a very different way, there will be no Mrs Grundy always looming in the distance.

I am getting dreadfully teased about Edward. I am very glad to be able to afford them a little amusement. Poor dears,

55

if such a little thing amuses them they must be badly off for entertainment. I am going to ask Edward what his views on the subject will be. I rather think he will be very broad minded. He looked awfully amazed when mother said I could not go with him to see his books. Enough about my affairs and such like foolishness.

Yours ever   Helen Noble

3 April 1896   6 Patten Road
Wandsworth Common

My dear and helpful Friend,

The cup of bitterness has been drunk even to the dregs. All is over and Father is at rest with Philip. He slept and knew nothing. No pain, no knowledge of anything. Like a little child he slept and never woke. It was as we had prayed to God it should be, He heard us and has granted our prayer. Mother was not there but sleeping peacefully with me, and when she was called it was over. Our cousin Charley, so faithful always to us, so brave and true, was with our dear one, and he heard him sigh gently and then silence.

The dear little mother so brave and strong 'til now became for a few hours quite delirious, and wanted to go to him, but it was best not, and after a few hours' terrible agony of mind, she slept. I have prayed all the time that when the end came I should have the strength for her. And again God was good, and she found help and strength in me, though what it cost me God only knows. She and I were by ourselves, for she chose me to be with her, and in all this terrible time it was a ray of joy, that after all she should want me.

On Tuesday we part with all we now have of our dear one. He is to be near us, in the little Cemetery at Wandsworth I think. We only have to live one day at a time. The thought of a future without him is too terrible. The little mother who is so weak must now be our first care, we must do our best to fill up in part (for the whole world could not wholly make up for her loss) the blank that is now left.

Your letter dearest child was indeed good and kind and helpful. Thank you and thank dear Aunt Emily too. His last

56

words were quite clear and it is our joy to know they were to the little mother. The doctor told her to go to bed, and father heard and opened his eyes and smiled so sweetly at her and said 'Good night, God bless you' as they always say every night.

The nurses have both been very good and kind and the doctor a hero. We all love him dearly and so did father. He has been this morning and comforted mother like a woman.

Edward wrote him a beautiful letter. He never heard it, but we did and know if he had heard it he would have loved it, as I know he loved the sender of it. Edward's name was always on his lips, and it has made the dear boy very glad. I will show it to you some day, for I have it. Mother seemed to think that as the dear father could not have it, I had the next right.

Mary and Lance did not know till this morning. Poor little ones! they too are brave. Mrs Warner has taken Lance away for the day. Everyone is so good, so good.

I have not yet seen his dear face, but it is happy and peaceful. No trace of suffering. He looks Aunt Flora says ten years younger, and his face is as noble and heroic to look at as his life has been. As the doctor says it is not a mere splash in the ocean, his has been like a ship in full sail, often nearly wrecked but always brave and so overcoming all. Now he is in the port which he longed to reach and all is well with him. He has crossed the bar, and he sees his Pilot face to face, and his look is honest and true and good. I seem to see God stooping to kiss him and saying, 'Well done good and faithful servant, enter into the joy of thy Lord'.

Is all this sense? I know not. I feel dazed and my heart seems to be breaking, but I am trying hard to be brave. I have not cried, I think if I could I would be stronger and more help, but my eyes are dry and burning.

Let not our sorrow sadden your holiday dear child. The sorrow would have been double if he was now suffering as he did a few days ago. He was tired and now rests.

Much love from us all to all, and much much from me to you.

Ever your loving friend   Helen

Written while Helen was working at her first job as nursery governess, away from home.

24 August 1896   Rotherfield

Dear old Janet,

It really was awfully bricky of you to write me such a long yarn, when in the midst of such gaiety and pleasure. I would have written sooner had I been able, in fact have had several tries, but only beginnings, this I hope to finish.

You seem to have had a gorgeous time on the yacht, I can imagine it all. You madder than ever, cheekier, rowdier, jollier, much sought after by all, especially the males of the party.

And now you are up in Scotland having a good old spree there, and then to Berwick, and an unspeakably good old spree there too. You are a lucky beggar and no mistake.

And here with me the world jogs on as usual, and I am happy, but deadly homesick. Of course this sad time we have had heaps to do, and the days have seemed hours too short to get everything in. But now the worst is over and we seem to be getting out of the wood a little.

Some time, I hope at the end of the second week I go home for a few days, and I count the hours and rejoice inwardly as each day goes by. It *is* such ages since I saw any of them, and when Mary came two weeks ago, I felt that I could not stand seeing her go off to home and leaving me here. However we had a jolly time, and talked our heads off. You see old girl I have never been away from home before for longer than a month, and it seems so strange not to be all together for the Summer holiday, this is the first time one of us has been away. A few days ago I felt too utterly wretched for anything, it was after Mary had been here, and told me of all the home doings, and how they wanted me to join them all. How Mrs Webb [Helen's employer] stands me at all sometimes I don't know, she *is* so kind, if she were less so, at times when I forget things, it would not make me feel so bad. Do you know the agony of trying hard, really hard to do your best, racking your brain to think if you have left anything undone, and are satisfied and pleased to think there is nothing, then when it is too late it suddenly flashes on you, you ought to have done so and so at such a time, and you are reproved and all your trying is useless, and life seems hardly worth living. . . . Today I feel sure I have done all I ought to, at any rate my time has all been fully occupied till now 8.0 p.m., and when I go to bed and lie and think and wonder if in truth today has been as good as I think, I shall remember that Mrs Webb told me to do something, and I have not done it.

I had an awfully exciting letter the other day from Edward. You must know he and father had often talked of a book Edward was to write, father would preface it, and it was all to be lovely. So quite on his own account Edward sent I think twelve or more perhaps of his published papers to Blackwood's to see if he would publish them in book form, under the title 'The Sweet o' the Year' (Tennyson). For a long time he heard nothing, and of course expected his mss. back every day. What was his joy when the other day Blackwood wrote to say he would like to have the book, if his enquiries about its saleableness proved satisfactory. He also asked E. if he would send him his (E's) diary of fields and woods which he keeps to look at with a view to publishing it. Isn't it lovely? Edward is now busy copying out the diary, and we hope great things. I think it is splendid at nineteen to get your first attempt accepted by the first publisher addressed. Don't you? and even asked for more! He is going to inscribe it to the dear father's memory, the next to *me*! He will not get any money for the first. I hope Blackwood is honest. Mr Webb says he is a first class publisher, one of the best, so I suppose it is all right. Only I know as a set they are rather money grubbing and do not mind at times deviating a little from the quite honest.

I hear at times amusing bits about him. Mary generally in a post script puts something about him—P.S. By the bye Edward gets handsomer every day, we are all in love with him. or P.S. Irene and I are in love with Edward, and say you will be an idiot if you do not marry him! We should if we could!! etc. He is very fond of them too, and goes home a good deal, in fact I hear more home news from him than I do from my people, who are fearfully lax about writing. They say I get fatter, horrors! so as I can go out so little for exercise I draw the water up from the well, which is eighty feet deep to the water, and the bucket holds two ordinary buckets full of water. So it is hard work, and Mr Huggett laughs at me. I churn too which is even harder work. I am teased by the farm people about Edward, who get no end seemingly of fun out of us, and I enjoy it as well, and it is good preparation for my holiday, for at home I know what they expect.

This letter seems one long grumble. You see the 'Grief stricken grumbler' stage is not yet in its decline. How jolly it would be now to have you here to tease and laugh my 'blues' away!

Your old chum   Helen

After 1896 there are no letters from Helen until 1899, by which time Janet had married Harry Hooton. Janet was a witness at Edward's and Helen's marriage after which Edward went back to Oxford and Helen stayed on with Janet and Harry for some months before joining the Thomas family at Battersea where her child would be born.

29 December 1899   61 Shelgate Road
Battersea Rise, S.W.

My dear Janet,

I would have written to you long ago to thank you for the charming head flannel you sent me, but I did not know your Broadstairs address. I hope you are not very offended with me for delaying so long. Thank you ever so much for the flannel and your good wishes.

When are you coming here again? I hope you are not putting off your visit until the great occasion, which is now not a fortnight off. [Philip Merfyn Ashcroft Thomas was born on 15 January 1900.]

Mother told me she had seen you at Ramsgate, and you both looked very well and jolly. What ages it is since I've seen Harry, however he's simply got to come when *my* society will not be the only attraction.

We were of course very happy at Christmas time. Edward worked all day and I went to Church and played with the little boys and every now and then ran up to Edwy to make sure he was there all right.

Mrs Dapple sent me a most lovely cot cover in blue and white, made of course by herself. I was so surprised and delighted Mater [Edward's mother] gave me, or rather the babe a huge cozy white shawl so that I think what with the head flannel and shawl and coverlet my babe did very well for Christmas presents. I am beginning to feel most awfully excited about it. I think of it all day, at least when I am not thinking of Edwy, and at night I nurse Edwy's arm and pretend it's a baby. And when I kiss Edwy's hand which is the baby's face, he thinks it is because I love him. Isn't he a stupid old thing to think I care twopence for him. As if I should kiss his hand! Oh dear me I am quite too silly for anything. I shall utterly demoralize poor solemn Dr Biggs. The babe and I will simply laugh and make fun of him all day.

Please give our love to Harry and to yourself.

Your loving old pal   Helen

Merfyn is now four years old and Bronwen getting on for two.

29 June 1904   Elses Farm

The Weald, Sevenoaks

Dear old Janet,

A few mornings ago, after dreaming of you all night I woke up with that lyric of Rossetti's and your tune for it, running in my head. And as I dressed and murmured the song 'I have been here before' all sorts of memories came crowding into my mind; hours spent with you, and incidents in my life in which you shared. And I remembered our wildness and enthusiasm, and our hopes and desires which we talked over so often. And I was glad that my dreams had led me to such pleasant places. Do those days seem good to you now I wonder, or does it seem foolishness that you and I, who are so far apart now, should have planned together these present days; should have talked of our lovers before I at least had one, or dared to hope for one; and our children when it seemed a light, pleasant thing to be mothers. And so it is pleasant, it is the most glorious thing in the world, but Oh

61

the pain, and the care, and the responsibility. We did not think of that! how could we when we had no conception of any of those things. We did not know that in all life's sweetest, most desirable emotions, pain is inseparably mingled, nor would Love, or motherhood, or wifehood be so precious were the pain not there. When are we going to meet again, you and I, the little, wild, loved impulsive Janet, and I the fearful, and shy and unconfident Helen.

Here we have an ideal house, with large, light rooms, and big country kitchen, and the loveliest country all around. We spend our time in the hay fields now, and both my babies are as brown as berries and as well as possible. Baby walks now, tho' she is a little timid. The farm yard is a Paradise for Merfyn. Edwy too likes it, and I hope will be well here. He is looking forward to seeing Harry, who will tell you all about it afterwards. I wish you could come soon. Oh I do so wish it.

I am busier than ever, and indeed when at the end of the day I consider all I have done, I wonder how I managed it; and there is always something left undone.

I can't write letters nowadays, but I had to write this, tho' it's you who owe me a letter. Still I know just how it is about letters, so don't bother. Harry will tell me how you are, and all about the babies. Do you know I am going grey as fast as I can; at thirtyfive I shall be as grey as a badger.

Goodnight old friend. Come and see us some day. Surely we did not say all in those far away days. Now we have real lovers, real children, to talk about. Goodnight Janet.

Your old chum   Helen

9 January 1908   Berryfield Cottage
Ashford, Petersfield

My Dear Janet,

It was nice to have a letter from you, for letters now are such a boon. I read them over and over again for company's sake, and get out of the shortest, dullest sort of letter an amount of pleasure and satisfaction that would astonish the writer. People—especially Mary, Irene and Mater—have been very good to me in this way; and there's one thing to be said about writing letters to me, I always answer them, for my one delight in my lonely evenings is pretending I am talking to this one or that, and I can pretend best with my pen in my hand. Of course my best letters are from Edwy, and never have I had such cheerful healthy sounding letters from him, no never since I have known him. It's simply glorious the good he seems getting, not only from the air, and the sea and the beautiful country, so wide and free, but also from the dear people who are being so kind to him; the people so different from humdrum me, and the number of them, and their light-heartedness, and their unconstraint. And not only because the sea is what it is, and the air, and the people, but because the whole is different in every detail from life here; and I think a downright change like that is good for everyone, especially for Edwy. I wish sometimes that I might go and renew my youth in that gay kindly family; but at present I am filled with a deep content, a glad thankfulness that all is so well with my dear old boy. Every day he surprises us—I and the children laugh at his strange doings: dancing, playing whist, having Molly and Chub in to tea and getting on splendidly. My only fear now is that lack of funds will prevent his staying there till he's done the book [*The Life of Richard Jefferies*]. We are very hard pressed at present, and of course it is an expense but I daresay he'll manage it somehow. He seems so hopeful about his book too, and the writing of a book is generally accompanied with groans of despair, fits of depression, fits of anger. Let us hope the book will not suffer, but I'm sure it won't. Do you think I feel a bit jealous of the Aldis's, the Webbs, the cottage, the sea, the air, the everything that has so soon worked wonders with him? Well I do a little. I would have liked after all this while of vain striving to have felt that I had had a finger in the pie. He is my whole life, my love in whose existence I exist and yet I can do so little, so very little for him. I know that a lot of the spirit in me is gone, and I had been a far better, wiser, more helpful wife if I had not let him mould me as he liked. One can love too well. But I don't know why I drift like this, it's foolish and useless. And just now my heart is filled with a great hope that this change may be a turning point, and that with a body so strong and healthy he may return with at last the confession

and Harry between you, will decide that life here in England on a small income (and I'm sure with all Harry's enterprise and practicalness and both your brains combined—the income would not be a small one, any way not so small as we have lived and been happy on for ten years) is worth over and over again riches in Brazil, cut off from all ties; especially for Harry who is such a very home loving creature. With all your combined qualities what a jolly, healthy joyous life you could lead—you writing and teaching, Harry poultry keeping, gardening and all kinds of allied industries. I personally cannot understand the point of view of anyone who thinks that such a life, such a splendid life for one's children could be bettered. I do hope and hope you will decide not to go, and let Harry work out his own salvation and yours too in a life full of so many possibilities of happiness and health and interest. I feel awfully deeply about all this, because I love you both so much and tho' it's no business of mine, I can't help saying what I feel, or a bit of it anyway.

Well, as to ourselves we are flourishing. We've never been rich or even well off, so we can look forward quite calmly to an income just enough and no more. Our children are having a quite perfect childhood, going to what we think is the best school [Bedales] preparing in every way we know of for a good man and womanhood. We are all very well indeed in our hill top house with its beautiful view over the vale to the great restful downs. Every day in my heart a great wave of thankfulness comes for all this life holds for me. And now especially, with my babe knocking every day to tell me he's all right and longing for me as I for him; and my breasts full already of milk for him, as if to tempt him out of his hiding place. I still teach at school, and so earn the children's fees, and do my five miles every day, and twice a week ten miles and half of that up and up and up a great high hill. Then in the holidays I am to have two Anglo Indian boys here who will pay me well, and so things go on, a hard pull sometimes, and then a time of rest, but always life, life, life. You know I've had a queer sort of life in a way, full of dark shadows, too dark many of them for speech, but on looking back the brightness is so bright that my life has been like a field of gold I see, and where little clouds freck the gold, the brightness

65

at the edge is brighter than anywhere. The children are splendid. Such sweet strange creatures, so different, each expressing
a quite opposite point of view. Bless them, how they will rejoice when they hear of what is to be theirs in the summer.
Edwy is well too, he grows stronger every year, and does
better and better work. It's a good thing I'm so simple a sort
of creature, when his nature is so complex and difficult. What
times we've had! What rapture, what despair, and always our
love absolutely undisturbed, like a great beautiful placid bird,
spreading its wings over us.

I'm *so* busy, for of course I'm away from eight o'clock
when we start for school, till 11:30 or 12 when I return.
Then there's lots waiting for me to do, and just now of
course *piles* of sewing. However I'm getting on, and shall
soon have my baby things finished. Then I have to make
things for myself—nightgowns, a dressing gown, all kinds of
things, and Bronwen too has to have a lot of things for next
term. I never have a minute. Everybody says how well I
look, and I'm just bubbling with health, and happiness. This
baby is a great beautiful present Edwy and I are making to
each other, he ought to be very extra lovely, he starts from so
much of beauty and happiness and calm after storm.

Well, well, here I go jabbering on, and friends are coming
for the weekend, and I've got heaps to do. So farewell dear
old girl. Love to you all, and to the Webbs when you see
them.

Ever your old pal   Helen

TO EDWARD, IN WALES

[Sepetember 1910]   Wick Green

Dearest one,

We were all up early today for breakfast at 7. It was so very
misty that I was half afraid the weather had changed, and
that we should get fine rain, but now at 9 o'clock the sun is
coming through and I think it's going to be hotter than ever.
Bronwen, Merfyn and Edith went off in good time, and I
have just watched the train steam across the valley. Bronwen

was very excited and pleased to be going, and coo-eed joyously to me at my bedroom window. Merfyn and Edith are driving up with Fox who is going to take me a little drive for a last treat for Nurse, who I have just paid, and wished I could have given her more, she had been so particularly good. However of course I quite see we can't, so don't think I'm feeling anything about it. I'm very sorry you are again poorer than you thought. How is it you get your accounts so wrong, and always on the bad side.

I'm thinking of you today with Gwili and so is Merfyn. He *has* so wished he was with you—Wales is a real love and a strong feeling with him, and we have been trying to sing Welsh songs together. I wish he could learn the language. How nice if we had a Welsh speaking servant, a pretty smiling Welsh girl with a beautiful figure and complexion and large white teeth. Oh but where would poor old Helen be then, always beside such a fair Eluned or Megan!

Your parcel came at dinner yesterday, and as I had had a lovely letter by the morning post, I did not open the parcel thinking it only soiled clothes. So late at night when I opened it, your letter was a lovely surprise. I'm glad you and Arthur [Arthur Ransome] managed at any rate to part friends. I was half afraid something might happen, and think you must have had yourself under good control to avoid a quarrel with one so absolutely antipathetic (is that the word?). It was a lovely letter just as I was going to bed, tired rather after a busy day; with that description of your slow walk and feeling so content dear. *Nothing* makes me happier than to know of such moods with you, and if only it could be oftener that life is so restful and careless for you, how good it would be!

Yesterday we took our tea to the slope of Wheatham, and enjoyed the soft misty afternoon, tho' the midges tormented us dreadfully. The children had the cart, and were letting it run with them in it down the slope by its own weight. They had one or two tumbles, but there was great laughter over it. Merfyn, Baby, Peggy [Digby] and I are going again some day soon. It's as far afield as we can go down the lanes, for they are so rough that we cannot take the perambulator, but have to carry Baby, who is too heavy for me to carry far.

Weeding is very difficult now, the ground is so hard and

dry, and a little rain would do good, tho' these days of sun and peace are delicious.

By the way that piano of Miss Wells is very cheap, for it's a good one. Could we beg, borrow or steal the money. It *would* be lovely to have it, and it's such a chance of a really good piano.

Merfyn and I will feel very strange tomorrow when he and I and Myfanwy are alone, I think we shall like it; for he is most devoted to his little sister, and loves to be where she is, and is delighted when he can hold her a minute or when she smiles at him. Her smiles are fascinating now, and she *almost* laughs. We get soft little coos sometimes and she tries hard to express her content and health in sounds. Everybody is amazed at her intelligence and size and general forwardness. She is three months old as far as everything goes except dates. She will be four weeks on Tuesday.

I had a nice letter from Mrs Little. I'll send it. You see William Davies keeps her well posted up in our news. Isn't it funny about the one unreadable chapter. How proud he is of it, and I expect it's very *very* mild, tho' no doubt there are many really unreadable chapters in his life; but his sense of propriety is so delicate, and his reserve so deep rooted that I don't think the public will get from him anything both quite true and quite unreadable.

Well dearest I long for you home again, and yet while the lovely weather lasts I want you to have all of it to spend in that perfect happiness, and I'm afraid at home you cannot get it quite so well. I want you to get full of it and then perhaps you would keep it always. So don't hurry back dearest, *do not*, but come when you feel home is best for you, not till then.

Farewell sweetheart. Merfyn sends kisses and Myfanwy will give you hers when you come back—a baby's kisses are too soft and tender and sweet. Her open mouth groping on my cheek gives me I can't say what pleasure, it is almost a pain of happiness to feel her oneness with me, her absolute dependance on me, and her knowledge that it is well for her that she has me. Farewell dear heart. Ever and wholly I am yours   Helen
Love to all at Waun Wen.

10 November 1911   Wick Green

Dearest one,
    The children and I have just got back. I have been to Miss Simeon's where our reading developed into a furious argument between Miss Simeon and Miss Townsend on the new aspect of the suffrage question that the government have dropped this thunderbolt in the form of a manhood suffrage bill. Then I called for the children and we walked home together, in the very dark and cold night.
    It's been bitterly cold all day, very raw and cycling my hands and feet got numbed.
    It's the violinists' concert tomorrow, and of course I'm not going. I can't afford ten shillings, and so arranged for some children to come to tea. Then to my great disappointment I heard that none but strictly Bedales people were to be allowed to hear them at Bedales on the Sunday—not even Mrs Fish, Mrs Badley's great friend. So of course I knew I could not go. But today I met Mr Powell who told me that Mrs Russell had especially invited me, and that I alone of outsiders am to go at her special request. She of course is the promoter of the whole affair. Isn't it nice of her, so I shall hear the music after all, and I do so love it.
    I did not tell you did I that Mrs Scott has asked me to go next Thursday morning to see the drawing classes. She says she considers both the children very good, and Bronwen exceptionally so, particularly in her observation of small details of plants, twigs etc. So I am going. Mrs Scott asked me to thank you for your letter.
    I saw Merfyn boxing the other night and he seemed to be doing very well. Mr Scott said he was a long time getting into it, but he's very pleased with him now. And tonight Merfyn tells me, he knocked his opponent into smithereens. They are both very well, and happy, and just as keen on school, and not too tired when they come home.
    I had a letter from Sarah Ann today thanking me for some things I sent her. Her mother has been very poorly, but is rather better. She sends her love to you.

69

I also heard from Mrs Unsworth. They have let their house for the Winter, and are going to Spain and Algiers and she wants me to go and see her. The other day at breakfast Maud was in here, and she saw Mrs Lupton come up from the wood in her nightdress and overcoat. She said, 'There *are* some funny folks about, if the old people could rise from their graves, *wouldn't* they see some comic cuts?'

The other day we were talking of designs for stamps for Merfyn's 'island' and then got on to talk of the typical animals of the country apropos stamps. I said the English stamp ought to have a dog on it, Merfyn said the Welsh a sheep, and Bronwen said, 'And the Americans a Teddy Bear', which I thought quite smart.

The MacTaggarts are quite nice people. He is a typical Scot, *very* Scotch—tall, grim looking, not much humour. She is short and plump and half German, plenty of humour, and quite clever I should think. They've heaps of money, he's a retired Burma rice merchant, and for the first time have they and their children really settled altogether in a home of their own. I liked them both.

At meals I've been reading Pepys Diary which I like most awfully. Is it complete here, or expurgated? I only have meal times to read at, I sew on all the evenings I'm not writing to you, and I'm gradually working through my pile of mending and making. So a diary just suits that sort of time. Wells' book I liked, but feel it dissects too much all the time. It is very interesting and the character of the girl (Miss Pember Reeves I suppose) is very fascinating. But the book is not nearly so good as *Tono Bungay*.

I do hope you are sleeping better, and that you are cheerfuller. I don't like the thought of your being alone so entirely, but of that I suppose you are the best judge. But I can't help thinking it would be best if you could when you wanted to drop in on a congenial friend.

By the way I should like to see if it comes your way that poem of Masefield's reviewed by Wuff today. His novel *Multitude and Solitude* felt awfully unreal and wishy washy after Wells. I simply could not read it. Cobbett, or Pepys or Wells, real people talking about real living and real life, that's what I like in books. *The Story of my Heart* too because it is so full of life and experience. But most modern novels sicken me with their unreality. Masefield's poem may be good I thought, the Wuff review is enough to damn it for evermore.

Well, I wonder if you are right about my being unable to be strictly economical. You are quite right about the twelve children and £2000 a year. But I can't cotton on to the red faced husband with an embryonic paunch. My idea of a husband is tall, thinnish, handsome (sometimes ever so handsome) fair, and tho' not red, certainly not pale. But the best of him is his smile, and with twelve children and £2000 a year he'd often be smiling. Oh I do love him when he smiles, it sets everything right, and if everything does not want setting to rights, it makes me ten years younger and more in love with him than ever, which is saying a good deal I can tell you. I'll forgo the dozen children and the £2000 a year, but I must have you and only you; just you with us happy and smiling and laughing. I could not be happy with red faced paunchlet, I hate the sight of him. I'd not touch him with a barge pole.

Don't work too hard at the Borrow. What is Mr Wilkins and how comes he to have Conrad, Meredith etc. in his shelves?

Have you seen any pretty Welsh girls yet?

I wish you could bring a nice little cockle donkey back with you. *Do.*

Do write to Bronwen. She's expecting a letter by every post. It's my letter day tomorrow. I hope there'll be some people in it. Churches and pilgrims and old farm houses are all very fine, in fact I like them when you've been there to warm them a bit, but best I love children and animals and people and girls and boys, and I like you among them better than all alone among mouldering things.

Baby is lovely, only she's got a large dark bruise on her cheek where she bumped into a corner. She says 'dada' when she sees the picture of a man, so she does not forget yet what a 'Dada' is.

Well it's bed time now, and I suppose I must go. So goodnight. How late do you sit up? You write to me early in the day I suppose, for I get your letters the following day by the first or second post.

When you think of me what is in your mind. How am I to you. I often wonder if I should know myself if I could look at myself through your eyes and mind. Goodnight sweet heart. It's a still night, but Oh it's far away from you. Farewell. If you ever smile when you think of me well that's lovely, but do you? Answer *all* these questions.

Goodnight. You're pretending to be too deep in your book to look at me. Goodnight. Ever and wholly I am yours.

Helen

TO EDWARD

[16 December 1911 (approx.)] Wick Green

Dearest One,

Only a few lines hoping this finds you as it leaves me at present, very well thank you!

There is no news except that there are only four days to your homecoming. And that when you get this there'll only be three, unless you count Tuesday itself as 31 days. It will seem a month of wet Sundays from getting up time till starting off to meet you time. The children and I may meet you, that is if I can find time. I daresay I'll stroll down to the station, but if I am not there, I daresay I shall have gone to the McTaggarts' for tea, so in case I am otherwise engaged I've told Maud to make tea for you, though if you like to wait supper till 7.30 or 8 I'll be sure to be home then. The McTaggarts are so very nice, and have asked me to go, and as *nothing* is happening on Tuesday after all the gaieties of the term I thought it would be a good opportunity.

I cannot answer your two last loving lovely letters, it's no good trying. I did not get *too* wet and cold in the hailstorm, but I'm very grateful all the same for the warmth and cheeryness of the sun after it. You see it's intoxicating me somehow. I'll be as mad as ten hatters by Tuesday if this sort of thing goes on.

I'll air your clothes for you, and get out the sweater and the old mac. (There's some wedding cake for you which I did not send on.) I've put the notebooks in your letter chest, and locked it. I paid the bills and have got receipts. Baring wants £8 all at a fell swoop, but it was a glorious debauch of bill paying and receipts reaping.

The children go to Bedales with the School to see *A Midsummer Night's Dream*. They won't be out till 9 o'clock, and of course I shall be there to meet them. I'll keep their books hidden.

I'm so glad old Borrow is done and that we are a yard or so further than you thought from the workhouse. I'm not sorry you have left Llaugharne. Those singing, running, pale girls with creamery voices who pass the windows of hardworking, handsome young married men fifty times a day, don't do it for nothing I'll be bound. Oh no. You're better at home with your old woman, who once ran and who once passed your windows as often as she could, and sang too when she'd a mind to, but who was never pale nor creamery (not that I think much of either quality in young girls), but who kissed you before you kissed her (was it yesterday?). Cream or no cream girls are pretty much the same all the world over, and I'd not give a snap of the finger for one of them passing your windows while you are bending over your Borrow (forsooth). Sit there with one eye perhaps on your book, but the other wanton eye looking for cream and roses and what not while the hussies pass before you that you may the more rove after them. Even so the hailstones may have got into my heart, but if they did the warmth and foolishness they found there soon changed them into magic wine 'which maketh glad the heart of man'. Well, don't expect me at Petersfield will you. Oh, but do expect Myfanwy who I daresay will go by herself *on her own two legs*.

For yesterday at the Bedfords' she walked from Molly Bedford to me with a delicious little chuckle of delight and pride, and then again a step or two.

Not a single line or word more till Tuesday. I'm so excited about my tea party at the McTaggarts'. It will be jolly won't it? Give my love to Mother, and tell Julian I'm sorry he can't come, and kiss your father for me, because I must let out somehow and that seems to me quite a good way. Good luck in town, and the best of luck at home, and a *sensible* wife, not the scatter brain creature I half expect you've got. Anyway such as she is she's yours,   Helen.

6 August 1913   Yew Tree Cottage
                                                          Steep

My dear Janet,

Thanks for the tea. Here's 7/- for it and its postage.

We are in our cottage now, and we love it. It's awfully cosy and pretty and I love doing all the work. I expect you along with everybody else wondered what sort of job I should make of it, and shook your heads over it. Well, I felt that and I am just determined that it shall not fail through fault of mine. I keep it beautifully clean and tidy and have great joy and pride in it. It is I who am making a home for Edward, the only time I've had it all in my own hands, and I believe it's going to be the happiest home we've ever had. I know I shall do my best, and my dear old boy is trying too. Yes! Isn't he handsome but he's more than that. I've never met a man who could come anywhere near him in looks or in character either. If only he had a little more native hope and joyousness, so that all this bitter discouragement and anxiety had not driven him to despair. But I don't give up hope, I feel he *must* come out all right. He's tried hard during these last two years to kill my love for him but it's just the same as it always was, it's my great treasure, the thing that keeps me going, that is my life, that and the children. In my heart I have memories so splendid that I am rich in happiness tho' I spend so very many days of utter misery. Sometimes I think he does not love me any more, and my soul gets into a panic of terror, and then out of the darkness comes some wonderful gleam that gives me new hope, new life, new being and I start again. And now in this cottage it's all going to be easier. Even Edward's mother so doubtful at first often is hopeful now after seeing it and seeing that I'm not as bad as she thought. The fact is that nobody in this world but my sister Mary knows me at all. I'm too simple and primitive in many things and too sensitive and morbid in other ways, and everyone even Edward makes the greatest mistakes about me. I'm like my mother a little, but more like Father, but it absolutely surprises me how people mistake my motives and my reasons and my point of view. I'm grateful for the bit of Mother in me, or else I had been crushed absolutely flat by now. I couldn't have gone on, had I not her wonderful power of recovery, and did I not love people *all* people so much that I would not hurt them if I could help it by showing how hurt I was. I often and often feel utterly lonely, and I *am* very lonely, for there is not one soul I know except Mary who really cares for me, and who tries to understand me, or thinks it worth the bother. I have lots of good friends here, but they just know my social side (for I have a terrific social instinct like my mother) but I'm still lonely, and often cry and cry in my solitude.

Oh well, life's not the easiest thing in the world is it? Goodnight.

Ever your pal,   Helen

TO ELEANOR FARJEON

Friday night [October 1914]   Steep

Dearest Eleanor,

One consequence of your not telling me this joyful news [Herbert Farjeon's marriage to Joan Thornycroft] is that I am worrying you with these affairs, which had I known I would not for the world have burdened you with. So there! Isn't it just splendid. I feel it so deeply, I don't quite know why; at least I do, there are so many reasons. I wrote very impulsively to Bertie, and have had a sweet note back which has made me so happy. I was not sure that he would believe my gladness could be sincere seeing I am so far away, outside, beyond him and his world. But I think he did feel it. Anyway I had to say it, and it was kind of him to acknowledge my nervous little word.

Now dear about all you have done for me. The parcel has not arrived yet, but will tomorrow I expect, then I must set to work and dress the doll, for which thanks, as thanks for all.

About the watch which is really Edward's concern. He's disappointed you've got one so cheap, and asks you if you could get another better one, spending all the 15/- and going up to £1 or 25/- not more. Edward has 5/- of Bronwen's, and 5/- he wants to put himself and get her a good watch. I'm *so* sorry about it. It was my fault, for I thought a cheap one would be good enough for her. But he hates the idea of anything cheap. Selfridges will I'm sure change it, but I wish I had not to trouble you about it. The same kind only better is what he wants.

Now as to blouses. I think the pattern charming. It's just what I like, and I'm in love with it. But my dear it's too lovely and dainty and unwashable to work in, and I'll just make it into a tunic as you suggest for afternoons, and to wear with the new skirt I'm going to make, to go with the new coat. Edward likes it too, *very* much. But you see there's still the morning blouses to consider, so you must not be hurt or foolish, but just let me buy either this woollen crepe, or the cotton blouse stuff you mentioned before. For I *must* have morning blouses, and I should have to buy stuff, and I can't let this tunic idea go, it pleases Edward so. So there you are. So be a good child and tell me how much it is and please let me buy it, for I can't send it back, and I shan't have my working blouses either.

About the coat, you are an angel to take such trouble, but I can't make up my mind. I yearn after the 18/11d. of course, but I really don't know what to do, for it's no good spending 12/11d. and then it's going loose and bad shaped and making me look sixty instead of fifty, and awful at that. I pore over illustrations and can't persuade myself that the 'serviceable' coat at 12/11d. is anything like as good, or will do at all when on the next page I see the 'smart' coat for 18/11d. However, ever and ever so many thanks for your dear help.

Tomorrow, tomorrow, tomorrow. My love and my heart is with you all. Having known the greatest joy that was ever known, after such a beautiful growing into love as ever was, my whole soul goes out to them.

Good night now.

Ever my love is yours   Helen

I return the P.O. 7/6 and Edward says any extra you spend up to 10/- will you spend and he'll repay by cheque having no cash just now. Edward likes the woollen crepe *very* much, but it's too lovely for working in, so please let me buy the cotton from you. *Please*. The doll is perfect.

4 April 1917   High Beech
                                                              nr. Loughton

My dear Janet,

How I should love to accept your invitation but just now
it's quite impossible and I'm most dreadfully disappointed.
Irene is here now and will be for another week, then Margaret
Valon is coming and then I have the little John Freemans
coming. So you see I'm fixed here. And anyway it's not easy
for me to leave home. I've got no nice Mrs Rodd to look
after things while I'm away—I don't know a soul here—and
tho' I have left Bronwen for a few days to mother Merfyn
and see him off at 6.45 (he has to have breakfast at 6.15 and
he and I get up at 5.30) still I don't like doing it and it's
never been more than a day or two at a time. So you see my
dear how it is. Sometimes I long to get away for a real rest
and change and I'll have to make some arrangements sometime for a little holiday, but my visitors make it impossible
now. Also I expect Bronwen will be away most of her holidays.

Ever so many thanks all the same. Myfanwy and I would
have *loved* it. I'm getting on all right tho' this terrible winter
will stand out in my memory as a sort of nightmare. The intense cold and the long dark days in this strange place, and
then on January 11th that terrible parting, not knowing when
we should see each other again; knowing nothing but that for
each of us it was so terrible that I did not know one could
live through such agony. But knowing so well our love for
each other and the deep down happiness that nothing can dis-
turb *has* made life possible, and tho' in those first few lonely
weeks I just existed from day to day doing my work and
trying to keep fear from my heart, at last something more is
possible, and our love for each other which has seen us
through so many dark times and over rough places is making
life possible now, real life I mean with happiness and laughter
and hope.

I hear very often from Edward, splendid letters full of his
work and his life and also of that absolute assurance that all
is so well between us that that is all that really matters come
what may. And I write long cheery letters to him, all about

77

our little doings and interests, and the children and the country, and for both of us the post is the event of the day.

I think he is just wonderful, doing his soldier's work as well as ever he can, and yet still the poet too delighting in what beauty there is there, and *he* finds beauty where no one else would find it and it's good for his soul and he needs it. He gets little time for depression, and so do I. That awful fear is always clutching at my heart, but I put it away time after time, and keep at my work and think of his home-coming. The real thing that matters is eternal, but Oh tho' my soul is perfectly content, my poor old body does want him. My eyes and ears and hands long for him, and nearly every night I dream he has come and we are together once again. But I can wait easily enough if only my beloved will come to me at last. If I *knew* he would come how easy would be this interval! Oh Janet how lucky you and Mary and all the other women I know are who have got their men safe and sound, I can't imagine what the war means to them. And yet I know how we do feel it all those fine young lives and all the terror and horror and vileness of it. And then too our pockets. We just scramble along somehow, I just making ends meet and wondering how I can do it next month when things are still dearer and what I can cut out next of our already so very simple menu and general expenditure. Isn't it difficult? But nothing matters to me I don't care how I have to work and manage and scrimp and scrape in fact I'm glad I have to do it, I'm glad I, like my dear man, have material troubles as well as those others, and if at the end he comes back to me safe and sound and we can start life again how worth while it will all have been.

And it will be a new start for him you know. The army at least provides a small income, not enough but something any-way. When he's out of it we shall have nothing and he will have again to make a place for himself and all the old struggle over again.

Well surely the end is in sight.

Thank you dear for thinking of me and Myfanwy. Give me another chance sometime. I get *so* tired for I do everything here, washing and all and never have a bit of help, and I'm not the quite untirable horse I used to be. Still, I'm game for a good bit more.

My dear love to Harry and the children and your dear old self from   Helen

[April 1917]   13, Rusham Road
                                                                    Balham

My dear Janet and Harry,

Before you see it in the newspapers I want to tell you that Edwy was killed on Easter Monday. You knew and loved him and he loved you both. I am trying to hold steadfastly to life and the realisation of the great peace that is in my soul and his too.

Mater and I are trying to comfort each other.

                                With love   Helen

14 May 1917   c/o Mrs Locke Ellis
                                    Selsfield House, East Grinstead

My dear old Janet,

It's only quite lately that I've felt able to write to any of the numerous friends who have written to me and helped me through these terrible days that so nearly were utter despair.

Here is country that he knew and loved and among friends in whose lives he had made an unfillable place a great peace has come to me. His great strong tender arms have lifted my soul out of despair, and he and I are one again, our love unchanged and eternal. Sometimes the pain comes back, terrible, soul rending, but it is as if he took my hand in his dear one and gave me fresh courage to live again the life he would have me live, happy and carefree with the children. I try to remember how rich I am in his love and his spirit and in all those wonderful years, and so forget that I am poor in not having his voice and touch and help. I *am* rich. What a man is mine, above all other men. How little he guessed dear boy what a place he had in the very hearts of his friends. He exacted all or nothing, and those who knew him loved him with a love surpassing anything I have ever known of. All kinds—men and women, great and small, rich and poor, clever and simple, they loved him as very few men are loved. And now because of their love for him it is poured on me. I am enfolded by it, Oh it is wonderful. I send you a copy of the letter his commanding officer wrote to me. It is above all letters precious to me in its simple sincerity and the characteristic picture it gives of my beloved. The very last letter I had from him was written the day before death came, and it was bubbling with happiness and eagerness and love. My God how rich I am in such love. 'He has awakened from the dream of life' and someday like the prince in the story he will kiss me to waking and we shall be together again as we never conceived, closer closer than ever we have been, one in body and soul, one in essence.

Janet dear I can't undertake the children. A great weakness came to my body, it failed me as it never had before, and I don't feel able yet to face my own little affairs and cannot think of taking on more than I have. Thank you for thinking of it, later perhaps I could but not yet.

I shall be in town before long, and will come and see you and old Hallow. May I? I want to keep in touch with all that he loved and that loved him, people and places and things, and you are our old old friends.

I'll write no more now dear. Goodnight to you both my two dear friends. Pray for me for indeed sometimes my courage goes and the way seems too far and lonely. Only sometimes because I get tired and full of pain, really he is so near me we speak to each other and I have but to put out my hand and he takes it. He is my all, my life, all all to me.

Helen

III / A REMEMBERED HARVEST

WELSH RELATIVES

NOT LONG after we were married, Edward took me to Wales to visit relations of his father's. The family I remember most vividly all worked in the tin-plating works in South Wales and lived in one of the quite new and very ugly villages on sites that a few years before had been wild mountain country, and still retained traces of beauty which one came upon unexpectedly. A stream flowed down from the mountain still uncontaminated in its upper reaches, though lower down chemicals and refuse degraded it into a sewer; wild bits of mountain with curlew calling and horizon unmarred by industry. The people too were countrymen though they worked in factories, and whenever they could went tickling trout or rabbiting, or just for love of the solitude and beauty walked out to picnic or explore. They still had their clear eyes and skin and glowed with health. They were not touched by the new ways and were in those days a most happy, independent, closely knit people.

The house in which we stayed was a grim-looking detached house on the edge of the village. It had been built by its owner and here he had brought his bride back from the country, to work in the factory, and here they had reared a large family of sons and daughters.

The ground floor of the house was divided into one spacious kitchen, a small parlour and a large scullery which also served as a bathroom. Here was the huge copper, always full of hot water, and the great tin bath, and here the men of the house, coming in at all sorts of odd times from their shifts, took their baths before having their meal. The door of the scullery stood open and lively talk went to and fro between the man bathing and the rest of the family in the kitchen.

I never got to know the relationships of all the people who thronged in this kitchen. But I knew they were sons and daughters and their wives and husbands, who did not live with their parents but who foregathered there and came under the rule of Mrs Hughes.

She was a very fat shapeless woman who had never been outside this village since her marriage. She was the head and centre of the family, even for the married sons and daughters.

83

She had been handsome and her hair was still jet black and her eyes bright. Her face was unlined and her complexion clear and unblemished and her strong teeth which she often showed—for laughter was natural to her—were even and white, though when I showed her my tooth-brush she roared with laughter, as she had never seen one before. In spite of her great bulk she was never idle. If she was not tackling a huge family washing-day, she was baking a batch of large crusty sweet-smelling loaves, or cutting thick rashers from the delicious home-cured bacon which was their chief food. Everything in this kitchen was on a large scale. The long heavy table scrubbed white, the giant-sized oval frying pan always on the hob, the enormous enamel teapot, its contents black and boiling, for food and drink were always ready for the men coming off shifts. A white cloth would be spread over the table and plates full of home grown food, meat and vegetables, would be put round; and to the noise of laughter and talk would be added the clatter of knives and forks and the clink of cups and saucers, for always tea accompanied every meal.

These meals used to terrify me because one was expected to eat so much. First of all the meat and vegetables, and before one had half got through that, a thick wedge of apple tart would be put alongside, and after that waiting to be eaten a plate of cake or slices of bread and home-produced honey. I looked along a line of piled up plates of food which it would offend not to eat, and my courage often gave out.

After dinner and all washed up, we would still sit round the table, or the men would, while Mrs Hughes carried in a basket full of white sheets and shirts and aprons which she damped down and folded in piles ready for ironing. Several irons were propped against the bars of the range now half-way up the chimney with glowing coals. This fire was never allowed to go out except when the chimney needed to be swept. The married daughters or sons' wives would call in for an after-dinner gossip. The same dark-haired and bright-eyed girls all with wonderful skins and gleaming teeth, and all with a tiny child at their skirts and an infant carried in the large flannel shawls wrapped round to make a kind of sling and then over the mother's shoulder and round her back, thus leaving her hands free and the baby safe and comfortable.

I sat entranced listening to their musical Welsh voices speaking their mother tongue, for some of these people could speak very little or no English. London was to them a fabulous place where the Queen lived, and they would ask me all sorts of questions about life there. 'And do you know Mr Rhys of London?' As it happened, I did! I remember their incredulous surprise when I told them there were no fairs in London, and in high falsetto notes one of the girls cried, 'Then where do you buy your flannel?'

It was summer and some of the babies would be brought in little short shifts scarcely covering their dimpled limbs. I remember Mrs Hughes addressing one of her infant grandchildren who had struggled from his mother's lap on to the kitchen floor under the table where he lay on his back playing with his toes. 'For shame our Thomas Traherne Thomas for showing your nakedness to the London lady.'

While we women were talking, one or two men, all black from their work, would come in, and Mrs Hughes would get up to fill the bath for them and get the frying pan replenished, and one of the sons would stoop down and pick up his son from the floor and toss him in the air and speak some endearing Welsh baby talk to him.

Everything in the house shone with cleanliness and polish. The linen could not have been whiter, the brass candlesticks—six pairs of them in graduated sizes on the mantelpiece—could not have been more shining, and the brightly coloured jugs hanging on the dresser could not have been more gay.

Mr Hughes was a tall spare man passionately interested in politics and hardly less so in his garden and his pig. His orchard was his particular pride and he got his appletrees from the very best nurseries. He was very proud of Edward and of his writing and liked to talk of the literary people Edward—whom he called Edwy—knew. I was Mrs Edwy. Edward had a lovely speaking and singing voice; though he could not speak Welsh he knew many of the Welsh folk songs and if he would sing one of them the pride and happiness in him were wonderful to see. If I shyly uttered some simple Welsh phrase, they would clap their hands with delight at hearing their language so badly pronounced.

We never sat in the parlour, which was hardly ever used except for ceremonial occasions such as a wedding or a funeral. Here the family Bible and family portrait album were kept, and the best black clothes for use on Sunday. The parlour housed a set of Chippendale chairs and other lovely pieces of furniture handed down from generation to generation, highly polished, unused and incongruous-looking among the gaudy pictures, wool mats and rag hearth rug, and fireplace filled with crinkled coloured paper. In front of the lace curtains were pots of geraniums, and a huge maidenhair fern stood on the Bible. Here the books Edward had written were kept with other family treasures. And indeed the room represented the family shrine, sacred and cold and stuffy.

But the kitchen was warm and homely and brimming with activity. I never saw or heard among all the young people who gathered there any disharmony. It seemed to be an idyllic existence of people still untouched and unexploited, simple and warm, grouped in families of hardworking happy affectionate people whose pleasure and skill in music was their passion. In that ugly village street there would, more often than not, be a band of men returning from their work, singing in perfect harmony one from among their fine heritage of hymns and folksongs.

W. H. DAVIES

WHEN Edward was looking over a batch of minor poets for review, he came across a small paper-covered volume called *The Soul's Destroyer* by W. H. Davies—a name then entirely unknown to him. The book, which was privately printed and issued from an address in the East End of London, contained a single long poem, and my husband was surprised and delighted to find that he was reading the work of a genius. He communicated his discovery to his friend Edward Garnett and together they went to see W. H. Davies at 'The Farmhouse'— a Common Lodging-house. This meeting and the enthusiastic review Edward had written of the poem, established a friendship between himself and Davies which resulted in his coming to stay with us at our real farmhouse in Kent.

Davies was a short, stocky, dark man, rather Jewish-looking but with a strong Welsh accent. He soon made himself at home with us and we all grew to love him for his keen appreciation of family life, his unaffected happy nature and his lively talk. Merfyn and Bronwen were very fond of him and he of them. His wooden leg intrigued them greatly, and on one occasion when we were walking with him down a lane and he called the children to the side to avoid being run over by a farm wagon, Bronwen said to him, 'It would not matter if it ran over you, would it Sweet William, because you are made of wood!'

This wooden leg got broken and Davies was anxious to obtain another, but had a morbid dread of any of the villagers knowing about it, or indeed about any of his business. So under Davies's guidance Edward made a sketch of an appliance which he asked the village wheelwright to make, without of course telling him its purpose. He made it perfectly to Edward's design and when the bill came in it was for: 'Curiosity Cricket Bat—5s. 0d.', the joke of which Davies enjoyed as much as we did.

In the evenings, over a pipe and a pint of beer, he told us of his life: of how he could never settle to a job as a young man; of running away to sea on a cattle boat to America where the plight of the wretched animals greatly distressed him, for Davies had none of the attributes one might associate with a tramp. He was not tough or callous or rough and his manners were gentle and sensitive, especially to children and animals, and in dress and personal cleanliness he was fastidious. I never heard him swear or use a gross word. His narrative went on evening after evening and Edward said, 'Davies, you should write this', and though Davies had never thought of writing prose, he set about the task eagerly, asking Edward's advice now and then.

When the book was finished it was all that Edward had anticipated, and a publisher was sought; but since Davies was an unknown author, his book was returned several times, until one publisher said he would take it if Davies could get some well-known writer to write a preface. This proved difficult, but at last George Bernard Shaw was approached and agreed to undertake it. Shaw suggested the title, but the whole inspiration of the book and the help given to Davies over it was Edward's. *Autobiography of a Super Tramp* was an immediate success.

Edward rented a little cottage about a mile from our farmhouse for 2/6d. a week and used one of the rooms as his study, and he proposed to Davies that he should occupy the rest of the cottage. For this we provided the bare necessities in furniture—a bed, bedding, table and chair, pots and pans, and here Davies went, living on the ten shillings a week which his grandfather, the skipper of a coal boat, had left him.

Davies had an intense dislike of anybody's knowing about his domestic arrangements. He hated the idea of drawing attention to himself and raising questions in the minds of his neighbours. For instance, if he had once been into an inn to have a drink, he felt obliged whenever he passed the inn to do the same, however little he wanted a glass of beer, because he felt the landlord would ask himself—Why doesn't he drop in? Is he offended? Doesn't he like the beer? Is he short of money?—so if he did not want a drink he avoided passing the inn, often having to make a long detour.

When we left the farm and Davies, after some time, wanted to give up the cottage, I wrote to him and asked if he no longer needed the furniture and odds and ends we had given him, could a maid of mine, who had married and was very poor, have them? Davies answered that having had no idea of what to do with the things when he left the cottage, he had bit by bit chopped up and burnt the furniture and buried the indestructible pots and pans! So there was nothing left for the young couple.

He moved now into a furnished semi-detached cottage. On the other side of the party wall his landlady lived, and in order to impress her with his suitability as a tenant, his piety and good character, he sang at the top of his voice, to be heard through the wall, a selection of hymns and pious songs which he had been used to sing in the streets when he was saving his little income to pay for the printing of *The Soul's Destroyer*. But whether his lusty rendering of 'Where is my wandering boy tonight?' and 'Cwm Rhondda' had the desired effect, no one will ever know. Davies told us this in all seriousness as a good diplomatic move.

He was now making a little money by his poetry, which Edward never lost a chance of praising. When we left Kent for Petersfield, Davies went to London. There he was rather taken up by high society and became very much aware of himself as a poet. Poets, he observed, often wore velvet jackets, so he bought one and wore it constantly. He had a flat over a grocer's shop in Great Russell Street which was furnished by him as he felt befitted a poet. He had heard that literary people burnt peat on their fires, and he felt it incumbent upon himself to do the same. He asked Edward's advice about this and where he could store the peat in his tiny flat, and Edward suggested teasingly that he should burn his books and stack the slabs of peat on their edges in the bookshelves. However, Davies ordered the peat and then was in an agony lest it should arrive when he was out and give rise to unwanted speculations from the shopkeeper below. So he stayed in day after day. At last the peat arrived, and having nowhere else to put it he arranged the slabs as a sort of hearthrug in front of the fireplace; having settled that to his satisfaction, he was free to go out once more. What was his dismay when returning home one day he found a crowd outside the house, people running up and down his staircase and smoke pouring from the windows. A spark had set his peat alight, the firemen had entered his room and were busy dowsing it with water: the whole street was interested and excited. This intrusion into his privacy was the nightmare occurrence which Davies dreaded above all others, and that was the end of the peat.

I went to see Davies in his flat several times, and once he apologized for a picture which was hanging on his wall. As I am very short-sighted I had not noticed it, but he explained to me that it was a picture which he himself thought very improper. It had been given him by the artist, Austin Spare, and though Davies considered it quite unsuitable, he felt he must hang it on his wall in case the artist called and asked, 'Where's my picture?' So if Davies was expecting a lady visitor or a conventional friend, he would take the picture down and stand it with its face to the wall; poor Davies was in a constant state of trepidation about the picture, which was always going in or out of grace.

In this room the bust by Epstein was a prominent feature. Davies told me that when sitting to Epstein and watching him repeatedly adding lumps of clay to the nose—which Davies already felt was much too big—he got very nervous and begged the sculptor to desist.

For all his naivety, Davies was no simpleton. He was a Welshman through and through, and was shrewd in his sizing up of people's attitudes to him. His pose of what was due to or from a poet was never paraded before his intimate friends. Nor was he taken in by flattery, and when rich and fashionable people invited him to their houses and showed him off at their dinner parties, he well knew that such things were not a tribute to his genius but that these people only amused themselves at his expense by putting the tramp-cum-poet in an alien setting. Davies became as bored with them as they with him after a time.

To our children he was always Sweet William, generous, gentle and good-humoured, and he remained our dear and delightful friend until Edward left for France. Davies commemorated this friendship in a moving poem to Edward's memory.

ELEANOR FARJEON

[*This memoir was written at Eleanor's death in 1965. A few months later, in August of that year, Merfyn died suddenly, soon after his retirement; and in the same month Arthur Valon died in his nineties—the husband of Helen's beloved sister Mary who had died many years before, in the late 'twenties.*]

FOR MORE than fifty years—only ended just now—Eleanor was a part of our family. In later years of course as our lives took on different shapes, her part in our family became less active, less intimate; but she never ceased to be the one who rejoiced with us on happy occasions or on whose sympathy and comfort we relied in sadness. And this is how it came about.

Edward had been staying with Clifford Bax and a party of young people among whom were Rupert Brooke and Bertie Farjeon and his sister Eleanor. In his letter he told me of this original and clever girl. He obviously liked her very much, and it had been arranged that she was to stay with us at Steep for a few days.

We lived then in a small workman's cottage, and the day before Eleanor was to arrive I spent in cleaning and polishing and cooking. I was a bit apprehensive about our guest, for I thought I should not come up to her expectations of what Edward's wife should be. But on the day she was to arrive I put the finishing touches to the house—a bowl of violets in her bedroom—laid the table for tea with homemade bread and cakes, and set out to meet her. Edward was at work in his study some way up in the beech woods.

I knew her as soon as I saw her walking with quick steps and an eager expression on her face. Her skin and hair and eyes were dark. The hair was black and done in a careless bun from which curling strands escaped. She looked very gipsyish in her bright cotton dress and thick walking shoes with a large rucksack on her back.

'You are Eleanor!' I said and 'You are Helen!' she replied, and from that moment all shyness and diffidence fell from me and I felt utterly easy with this girl—for though thirty years old she had the complete unselfconsciousness and eager enquiring manner of a much younger woman. She talked of Edward, and I of the children, and soon we were at the cottage. She loved the tiny house and flung her arms round my neck in her impulsive way, with which I was to become so familiar, to show how happy she was to be there.

Soon the children came in and Bronwen and Myfanwy found that she was the perfect companion for a child. She could draw and cut out all sorts of things in paper, she could sing and play all sorts of games and best of all could tell enchanting stories. No wonder they adored her. She loved them and never grew impatient of their constant demands.

For Edward and me she was just as perfect a guest. Her witty, vivacious talk and her eager appreciation of our simple ways made her the easiest person to entertain. Indeed the entertainment came rather from her than her hosts. For her abounding vitality and quick intelligence made her a match for Edward's talk, and I could see how they stimulated each other and how her wit delighted Edward and banished for a time his deep-seated melancholy.

Eleanor had a strange upbringing. She was the only girl in a family of four, all brilliant in their way. Her father—whose Jewish blood showed itself in Eleanor's features—was a Victorian novelist and her mother was an American, the daughter of a famous actor, Joseph Jefferson. Being a delicate child, Eleanor had received no conventional education and had never been to school. She often laughed at her lack of knowledge of history and geography and arithmetic, but her father's library had been her school and from this she had educated herself. She had read deeply and from a very early age was encouraged to write. Her eldest brother Harry, a tutor at the Royal Academy of Music, had instituted himself as the dictator of the Farjeon children. His rule had been of the kindest, but was unquestionable. And Eleanor at the time we met her had only just escaped from Harry's dictatorship and for the first time in her life was tasting the excitement of freedom. No wonder this world of men and women and the natural beauty of the earth intoxicated her sensitive imagination. She was another Miranda experiencing the brave new world. No wonder that her emotions were as uncontrolled and innocent as a child's, no wonder that she fell in love with

92

Edward. This I very soon discovered, for at the sound of his 'Coo---ee' calling across the fields as he came down the hill from his study, her whole being would become alert, her eyes shining and her expression assuming an expectancy most tender and deeply moving. I could not feel any jealousy of the girl's love for Edward. For one thing jealousy is not a part of my nature, and for another I realized the innocence of this inexperienced girl's emotion. She gave no thought to anything but the present and the rapture of being near the first man she had met whose mind kindled hers and whose affectionate manner fed her own unsatisfied heart, and who was moreover a man of great physical beauty with an elusive charm which made him beloved among a large circle of friends. Edward was aware of Eleanor's devotion, but with the most sensitive tact kept it at a light-hearted level which she happily accepted. This strange bond brought Eleanor and me very close and created in me a kind of motherly protectiveness, for I could see into what difficulties such an untried and impulsive nature might lead her.

For us three all was well. She proved to be a marvellous walker, though her quick step and her forward-leaning body seemed unsuited to the long tramps we took over rough ways. But she never tired and her interest in all that she saw—the flowers of whose names she was quite ignorant, the beech woods which were a feature of that countryside, the extensive views right away to the South Downs and the sea—filled her with a genuine wonder and ecstasy. Her comments on it all were fresh and came from a heart and mind uncontaminated by convention or insincerity.

Bronwen—then aged about ten—was shocked at Eleanor's ignorance of country things which she had learnt unconsciously. She set out to teach her the names of flowers and leaves, and set her examination papers to test what she had learned. And Eleanor was as eager to learn as to please the child and tried her best to win high marks from her earnest teacher.

Her stay with us for these few days was the first of very many such times, and she became familiar with our ways and grew to know the strange and difficult nature of the man to whom she gave her first love. In later years, when the war had come and Edward became a soldier and a poet, she was a

4 AUGUST 1914—ROBERT FROST

WE WERE to spend a long summer holiday with Robert Frost and his family. They had taken a furnished cottage in a remote hamlet in Herefordshire near Ledbury, and we had taken rooms in a farmhouse across fields nearby. Edward and Merfyn were already there, having cycled from Steep, and I was to follow with our two girls, our dog Rags, and a Russian Bedales boy, Peter Mrosovski, who spent his holidays with us. So on 4 August 1914, quite undeterred by the news in the morning papers that war between England and Germany had been declared, we set out on the long and complicated journey from Petersfield to Ledbury.

I forget if there was any unusual crowd of passengers on Petersfield station, but as we proceeded on our journey it was obvious from the crowds in the stations we stopped at that people were in a state of excitement. Families on holiday were hurrying home, reservists were being called up and soldiers recalled from leave, and everywhere the stations were thronged with trunks, kitbags and other luggage and with restless and anxious people. However, very much later than our scheduled time we reached Oxford. Here we were told to leave the train which, in the ordinary way, would have gone on to complete our journey. The station was in a state of chaos. It was now late in the day and I asked the station master when I could expect a train to Ledbury. He said he could not tell me, and advised me to stay the night in Oxford when I told him I had three children with me. But even if I had been able to afford such a thing, all available accommodation was filled, I was told by a man who had helped me with the luggage.

So we waited and waited, after sending Edward a telegram. At last a train came in and the station master told me it was at least going in the direction of Ledbury, so I and the children got in hopefully. After a slow journey with many stops between stations, we arrived in Malvern at midnight and here we were told the train would go no further. So out we all bundled, the children tired and frightened. I again found the station master and asked if a train would be going to Ledbury. He answered, 'Not tonight.' I asked him if I and the children

95

could sleep in the waiting room, but he was quite firm in his refusal. I asked him what he would suggest I do, but he had no ideas at all. All he knew was that I must leave the station. However, a kind and intelligent porter heard my story and said he had a friend who owned a cab and he thought he would be willing to drive us to our remote farm beyond Ledbury. The cab eventually came and our considerable luggage and the children were packed in and off we went. The country was entirely unknown to me, and I had not the least idea, as we drove off uphill in the darkness, how far away we were from our destination or in what direction it lay.

But I shall never forget that drive over the Malvern Hills which a huge full harvest moon lighted up like a stage set. Even in my distress and weariness I was entranced by the beauty of the scene and the silence and mystery of the deserted countryside, either in deepest shadow or brilliant moonlight.

Once over the Malvern Hills the country changed and became very wooded and gently undulating, and still the moon most dramatically lighted it for us. And before long we were in the lovely little town of Ledbury, silent and empty and sleeping. In the market square our driver stopped to ask a solitary policeman the way to the farm. He came over to the cab and shone his lantern on to the sleeping children and me.

'Who are you and why are you travelling at this time of night?' he asked suspiciously. So I described our journey from Petersfield and told him that I was joining my husband at the farm. He wanted to know who everyone was individually and when he came to Peter the Russian boy his suspicions grew to a certainty that we were up to no good. The fact that our friend Robert Frost, whom I had mentioned thinking his name would be known, was also a foreigner, did not help. However, after taking down all I had told him in his notebook, with some agonizing delays over the spelling of Mrosovski, he let us go, after giving the driver directions to the farm, which he told us was about three miles further on.

The driver went slowly along the last mile so as not to miss the house in that sparsely inhabited country and before we reached it I saw in the bright moonlight—Edward standing at the gate. So all was well. We had arrived.

In the morning we were able to take stock of our surroundings and found everything very much to our satisfaction. The farmhouse stood among large orchards in which were grown the choicest of dessert plums, each hanging in its own muslin bag to protect it from wasps, birds and insects. These plums had to be without blemish and of perfect shape. When they had reached perfection, they were packed for Covent Garden, each in its own cotton-wool-lined compartment. The outside of the farmhouse was hung with delicious fruit which we were allowed to pick—greengages and large golden or purple juicy plums.

We met the Frosts. Robert and Elinor and their four children—three girls and a boy. They had rented a very scantily furnished cottage standing in the middle of a field about a quarter of a mile from our farm.

Robert was a thickset man, not as tall as Edward, with a shock of grey hair. His face was tanned and weatherbeaten and his features powerful. His eyes, shaded by bushy grey eyebrows, were blue and clear. It was a striking and pleasing face, rugged and lined. He was dressed in an open-necked shirt and loose earth-stained trousers held up by a wide belt. His arms and chest were bare and very brown. His hands were hard and gnarled. He spoke with a slight American accent. Elinor Frost—in comparison with her husband—is only a vague memory to me. She had a rather nebulous personality and had none of the physical strength or activity of her husband. Housekeeping to her was a very haphazard affair and I remember that when dinner time approached in the middle of the day, she would take a bucket of potatoes into the field and sit on the grass to peel them—without water to my astonishment—and that, as far as I could see, was often the only preparation for a meal.

It was at once obvious that Robert and Edward were very congenial to each other. They were always together and when not exploring the country, they sat in the shade of a tree smoking and talking endlessly of literature and poetry in particular. When it was wet we all assembled in the Frosts' cottage; and as there were only two chairs in the living room we sat on the floor with our backs against the wall, talking or singing folk songs in which of course the children joined.

I say 'against the wall' but actually the walls were stacked up with ramparts of shredded wheat packets, tins of rather cheap sugary biscuits and boxes of highly-scented soap—the Frosts' idea of preparing for a possible siege.

The poet Wilfrid Gibson lived a mile or two away and Edward and Robert often visited him. But sometimes Mrs Gibson would not invite them in as her husband was in the throes of some long poem and must not be disturbed. This evoked in Edward and Robert an attitude of faintly contemptuous ridicule. Behind this lay a little honest jealousy, for Gibson was at this time a very successful poet whose work was eagerly accepted by the American magazines and highly paid, whereas Robert hitherto had had hardly any sort of recognition in America. On the whole however the relationship between the poets was friendly enough, and Wilfrid wrote a charming poem, 'The Golden Room', commemorating this time of their association.

We had not been there many days when the village policeman called on us and told us that several anonymous letters had been received at his headquarters, suggesting that there were spies among us. Evidently, we thought, the result of our midnight interview with the policeman at Ledbury, or of the villagers' suspicion of us as strangers who sat up very late at night in the Frosts' isolated cottage, and whose unconventional ways they could not understand. The policeman was, he said, convinced that the suspicions were false, but he said it was his duty to follow up any complaints from the public and to make enquiries. Edward of course took the affair as a joke, but not Robert. He was very angry and said, 'If that policeman comes nosing about here again I shall shoot him.' In the end Edward managed to calm him and we heard no more of it.

I remember another remark of Robert's which also surprised and distressed me. In the course of talk the Negro question was raised, and Robert said, 'If my wife and I were in a gathering and a Negro came in, I should immediately take Elinor out.' I cannot remember if the subject was pursued or if it was at once dropped.

I never became close to Robert as Edward was. To Edward he was an inspiration, and he and Robert could hardly have been more devoted. They had been drawn together by Edward's recognition of Robert's genius, when Robert had failed to make any mark in America. Edward's reviews of his early volumes of poetry published in England laid the foundation for Robert's success here and later in his own country. And Robert in his turn encouraged Edward—who had not then written any poetry—to think of himself as a potential poet, and thus in the last two years of his life to give Edward his deepest intellectual satisfaction and pleasure.

The month soon passed and we returned to Steep. The war had come and all our lives were to be changed. Robert and his family returned to America where he found himself famous, and Edward enlisted in the Artists' Rifles and began to write poetry. But there was no enthusiastic reviewer to praise his poems. No publisher would take them and only a few of his intimate friends thought well of them. He never saw a poem of his in print under his own name, just two or three under the pseudonym 'Edward Eastaway', which he himself had, with a wry smile, included in anthologies he was commissioned to edit.

D. H. LAWRENCE'S VISIT

I HAVE forgotten what I had expected D. H. Lawrence to look like, but I remember being very surprised and startled by the thinness and the pallor and the red beard accentuating both. He came, brought by a friend of mine, to spend a week-end at my cottage in Kent. I admired his work; indeed his coming was to me a great event, and I was excited and a little nervous in anticipation of entertaining the man who I felt might be the prophet who would save the world. For the war which was but lately over, and had taken my husband, had also destroyed all my old romanticism. I felt the world had taken a wrong turn, and Lawrence's books had made me hope that he was to be its saviour.

The first sight of him was a disappointment. He looked so delicate, and lacked a sort of rough earthiness which I had expected. As I became more familiar with him, I forgot the look of ill-health and was aware only of the clear burning of his eyes, and the intensity of his being; and he became for me the master as I had imagined, and I became his disciple.

I forget what we talked of, but I remember his outburst of anger, his voice rising to a high shriek, when in the course of a discussion about the trend of scientific discovery, my friend suggested that some day life might be generated in a test-tube. And I know the response in myself to all Lawrence poured out in a passion of hatred and ridicule on such a blasphemous idea. His laugh of derision was high and piercing, and there was something sinister in it: there was a hint of cruelty in it too. I heard this unpleasant tinge of cruelty again when he was most amusingly mimicking a psychoanalyst treating a patient. Lawrence sat in a chair, back to back with an empty chair in which the patient was supposed to be sitting, and in the role of doctor he asked intimate questions, and in the role of patient answered them, and enjoyed poking witty and biting fun at the treatment, which was becoming a popular subject for journalists. I know he prejudiced me for ever against psycho-analysis and made me feel the artificiality of it and the danger.

I remember his saying, in a more serious moment, that to become a journalist was to sell your soul to the devil.

The part of his visit I remember with most pleasure is the time we spent in the garden. I had made it all myself from a waste piece of ground, and it was beginning to grow up and acquire the mature look that cottage gardens in the country have. The cottage and the garden are one, and already my herbaceous border with its polyanthus and violas and clumps of delphiniums with great lavender bushes at the corner, and the apple tree on the lawn, looked as if they had always had the black and white walls of my Tudor cottage for a background. I also had a vegetable plot and a tiny orchard and a few fruit bushes. It was all on a very small scale, for even the surrounding hedge of maple and beech and hawthorn I had planted myself from seedlings brought from the woods.

I lost my shyness in pointing out to Lawrence enthusiastically what I had done and asking his advice about things to do. He was full of suggestions and entered into everything with the greatest zest. He told me to put groups of winter aconites under my flowering bushes, and to let a clematis montana ramp over a shelter I had made for Myfanwy to play in when it was wet, and he seemed to be as pleased as I was that a white bryony had sown itself in my hedge, and that a seedling of gorse was growing strongly in a corner. He borrowed some gloves from me and showed me how to prune the gooseberry bushes, teaching me with the most minute care what to do and why, so that I have never forgotten. In all this there was something intensely lovable about him—his deep interest in it all: not merely the polite interest of the visitor, but the real interest of a man who loved the earth, and to whom a plant or a flower or a tree was a living thing needing wisdom and skill, care and love.

We spent a long time pottering about in the garden, and though it is no longer mine, the hedge and the gooseberry bushes and the aconites are still there. The place is sanctified for me because once he was there and left his spirit there.

Myfanwy soon found out that he was the man for her, and brought into the sitting room one of her favourite books of Edward's for him to show her. It was a volume of photographic reproductions of Goya's pictures, and for an hour she sat on his lap, as he with the same absorption and interest that he had given to the garden, showed her the pictures, explaining them and pointing out to her the details that children love, while she settled herself against his arm. The pictures of war and bull-fights he would not let her look at. 'I don't like those pictures,' he said, and turned to others. The child was spellbound as she looked at the book, sometimes turning her solemn face up to his to look at the man who was making the pictures more fascinating than they had ever been. He did not tease or cuddle her, as so many would have done; his interest and the child's were for the time identical. There was no condescension, no pretence; the child knew it, and believed in him.

When I had put the child to bed I prepared the supper. I laid the table, then quickly began dishing up, tidied my hair, took off my apron, and sat down to serve my guests in my afternoon dress. Lawrence praised the food, and we talked of cooking in various countries, for he was a good cook and showed knowledge and appreciation of food. Then he told me that however simple the food was—and as he and his wife had been very poor, it often was very simple—his wife always changed her dress for the evening, and treated the meal with a little ceremony, which he liked; and he said he wished I had done that, for it was satisfying to see a woman make the best of herself. I felt abashed and was sorry I had not changed, as I had a very pretty dress, which afterwards I put on; this pleased Lawrence. We talked of clothes, and he told me that he liked to see well-dressed women. He hated to see a woman patting her hair, or re-touching her face, or adjusting anything. He liked her to come from her room looking her best, confident and poised. He told me that he had made a peach-coloured satin dress for Frieda out of one given her by a rich friend, and remarked, 'Unpicking a Poiret gown is like unpicking Rheims cathedral.'

During a talk about moral conduct apropos something which I forget now, I said, 'But how am I to know what is right?' And he said, 'Follow the first spontaneous impulse of your heart, and it will be right. The reasoned conclusion is almost certain to be wrong.'

The next morning, Myfanwy, armed with the Goya book, asked if she could go in to his bedroom and with his permission climbed under the eiderdown beside him; and when I took in tea, there they were, she in the crook of his arm, and he, now looking rather like Don Quixote, showing her the pictures all over again.

Bronwen was still at school and though hitherto she had been a most sweet-tempered child, easy to bring up and amenable to our simple way of living—for I was poor—at the age of sixteen or seventeen she wrote that she would not return to school. She became self-willed and intractable and I was at my wit's end how to treat her. She must of necessity be trained to earn her living but she refused to consider any career that I suggested. I spoke to Lawrence of my difficulties and asked if he could help me as he had over the pruning. He asked if she was good at anything at school, and I told him that her art teacher had commended her drawing. 'What is she interested in?' he asked then, and I answered, 'Clothes and young men.' 'Well,' he said, 'why not combine her talent for drawing and her interest in clothes and send her to learn dress design?' This seemed an excellent idea which I soon took steps to put into practice, and after a time Bronwen went to an art school. But it was no good and she left at the end of the first term with a very poor report. Young men had got the better of Art! However, she married very early and her charm and sweetness returned and all was well. But the kindness and interest of Lawrence in helping me and his sympathetic understanding of my difficulty brought back my hero-worship of which he was fully and kindly aware.

On our last evening, the friend who had brought Lawrence said, 'Our hostess is the maternal type, don't you think?' But Lawrence replied, 'That she is, no doubt; but much more is she the disciple.' I felt very self-conscious at being the subject of this frank conversation, spoken as if I were not there. At that time, when I was still trembling with despair after Edward's death, I took it all meekly; but later, when I was calmer, I asked myself rather indignantly, 'By what knowledge and authority did these vain men assess me so easily and put me in my category?' They are both dead now and I am an old woman.

Lawrence wrote to me a warm and gracious letter of thanks and said, 'I have talked too much, but you tempted me by your capacity for listening.'

I only saw Lawrence once after that for a few minutes, and when the other day I read in his recently published letters one mentioning his visit to me, I felt a deep pleasure in reading the words written to a friend of his: 'I have met Helen Thomas. I like her.'

MEN AND BOOKS

TO Edward two elements were necessary to his spirit: they were literature and what is called nature. He could not have been happy or contented or indeed have lived fully unless he could easily have access to unspoiled country where he could observe birds and clouds and flowers; or books to read. Not any books; for as a little boy his father encouraged him to read good books, and read aloud to him Hans Andersen and Grimm's Fairy Tales, and later *Bevis* and *The Gamekeeper at Home* by Richard Jefferies. Indeed Jefferies had a profound influence on Edward's life, at a very early age interesting him in the country and country life and sending him out of the suburbs where he lived to the country—as it then was— of Malden and Wimbledon to experience for himself what he had read about in the pages of his favourite author.

When I met Edward in 1896 I was nineteen and he eighteen —eight months younger. In March he caught me up and we were the same age till I leapt ahead in July. Edward had begun to write and it was this that brought us together. My father was a writer—an essayist and critic of some repute, and a noted encourager of young and ambitious but inexperienced writers. William Watson, Richard le Gallienne and Hall Caine were three of the young men who later made names for themselves, whom I remember meeting when we lived in Southport, and there were others. And now Edward was determined to write. His father, anxious to know if his eldest son's writing was of any worth, consulted the minister of the Unitarian chapel he attended, which was also our place of worship, and the minister suggested to Mr Thomas that my father would give the boy all the help and sympathy in his power. So Edward and I were brought together by literature.

My father thought very well of Edward's essays and notes about the country—the notes were minute observations of clouds and atmosphere, of birds and trees, of hills and streams, which showed extraordinary knowledge and intimacy with wild life on many planes. Edward's first book, *The Woodland Life*, published in 1897, was dedicated to my father who helped Edward in many practical ways with the book. My father was very delicate and not many months after Edward's first meeting with him, he developed the illness from which he died, and Edward lost an affectionate and understanding friend and a valuable critic and helper in the field of writing.

But he had by now decided to be a writer and to live if possible in the country. This met with strong opposition from his father, who by this time was quite out of sympathy with his unpractical son. Edward won a scholarship to Lincoln College, Oxford, and met there at Balliol and Merton as well as his own College a set of brilliant young men among whom were J. H. Morgan, E. S. P. Haynes and Ian MacAlister, whose influence only strengthened his determination to earn his living by writing.

At Oxford he discovered and possessed himself of the work of such men as Sir Thomas Browne whose *Urn Burial* and *Religio Medici* became favourite books of Edward's. Clarendon's *History* was another book he loved, also Camden's *Britannia* and Aubrey's *Brief Lives*. Indeed his reading ranged from Chaucer, through Elizabethan poets and dramatists and the eighteenth-century essayists and novelists to the romantic poets, among whom Shelley and Wordsworth were his favourites, and to Blake, Keats, Tennyson and Swinburne. His mind was filled with the excitement and delight of this unfathomable treasure of great literature, which he read over and over again, so that the writing of fine English became an integral part of his being. All his life he loved words and beautiful prose as well as the finest poetry. He knew the Greek and Latin classics too and would read them aloud to me, for though I could not understand them, the lovely sound gave me as much delight to listen to as it gave him to pronounce.

Edward preferred old things and many of these loved texts he had in very early editions bound in leather and with the lovely type and paper of an earlier and beauty-creating age. He possessed at one time lovely old copies of Sir Walter Raleigh's *History of the World* and Clarendon's *History of the Great Rebellion* and Browne's *Religio Medici* and these time-honoured volumes gave him intense pleasure to handle and to read from them rather than from modern and more convenient editions of these great works.

I had lived all my life among books, but I was not familiar with the earlier classic writers except Chaucer and Shakespeare who from early years I have loved. So Edward revealed to me two worlds of which I was quite ignorant, the world of nature and the world of poetry. I had always lived in towns in Lancashire and in London and had no idea of the life of the fields and woodlands, streams and moorlands. But strangely enough even as a small child I had felt an indefinable longing for something—I could not tell what. But it had to do with woods and fields and flowers and was something quite beyond my imagination.

Then, when Edward came to our house, my father, to whom I had never mentioned this vague longing of mine, but who with his penetrating sympathy knew of it in me, asked Edward if when he was going on one of his walks into the country round Wandsworth, he would take me. How excitedly I set out with him and how with such a companion the delight in everything we saw which he could tell me about, and the joy of at last being in the world I had so longed for, away from streets and houses and noise and ugliness, never decreased, and never has though I am now a very old woman.

Then on these walks which now became quite frequent, we spoke not only of what we were seeing and experiencing—I asking endless questions and Edward shocked and amused at my ignorance—but also of what we were thinking, what reading and thus it was that I was introduced to his beloved Wordsworth and Shelley. The first book Edward ever gave me was a rather ornately bound selection of Shelley's poems in a series published by Dent. I thought the little volume with its pale green cloth binding and its curiously new design in gold and its rather thick paper and wide margins a most lovely book, and when after reading to me from it he offered it to me as a present, I could not believe it. It has been all my life my most precious possession. Edward later, at my request, copied some of our favourite lyrics into the fly-leaves and there they are now, the ink rather faded and the handwriting youthful and immature.

Later Edward gave me a volume of Wordsworth in the same series, but though, when I grew older and more experienced in life and poetry, I admired Wordsworth deeply, even above Shelley, in my youth it was Shelley, with his ideas of rebellion and freedom who appealed to me and influenced me; also his lovely music and images excited me and filled me with ideas of living that I felt were daring and new, and I adored the man and the poet. Edward, who loved his lyrics, was never touched by Shelley's theories and ideas. His mind was always more mature, more discriminating than mine, and my romantic aspiration was sometimes disappointed to find he criticized what I thought perfect. Blake was a poet that we fully agreed about and my love and admiration for him has never wavered.

Edward became the critic of poetry in the *Daily Chronicle*, which in those days included a literary page of a very high standard. H. W. Nevinson was the literary editor. It was the time of a great outpouring of minor verse and the Georgian poets (as they were later to be called) were writing. Among these Edward was instrumental in 'discovering' Walter de la Mare, whose *Songs of Childhood* he found to his great delight in a parcel of very inferior stuff. He praised it and out of this first review arose a warm and lifelong friendship between Walter de la Mare and Edward. Other poets whose success was largely due to Edward's praise in the *Daily Chronicle* were Ralph Hodgson, John Freeman, Wilfrid Gibson and W. H. Davies.

A poet whom Edward admired above others was Thomas Hardy. Edward thought that Hardy's poetic genius far outshone that of the novelists, and I think he would undoubtedly have put him at the top of a list of contemporary poets.

Of prose writers of his time W. H. Hudson stood out in his estimation, and *The Shepherd's Life* and *Far Away and Long Ago* were two books he could hardly praise enough. A strange friendship—because hardly ever expressed—but one of deep understanding was created between these two reserved and solitary men whose love of the English country and its people was the great bond. Mr Hudson, whom I met only a day or two before he died, was stricken with deep grief when Edward was killed. He had tears in his eyes when he said to me, 'I loved him as my own son.'

Another writer whom Edward admired and whose book

Arabia Deserta he reviewed for the *Daily Chronicle* was Charles Doughty. I remember he was very excited about this author and explorer, and he and his friend Edward Garnett, who shared Edward's enthusiasm, did all they could to get the book talked about. But it was caviar to the general then —though now I believe it is regarded as a classic.

The last poet that Edward helped to his recognition in England was Robert Frost. Here again an immediate friendship sprung up between the two men and it was Frost who gave Edward enough courage and faith in his powers to become a poet.

And now when the Georgians are out of fashion, love and admiration of Edward's poetry still grows, and more and more people are drawn to the man and his world. No one would be more surprised and grateful than Edward who was killed in France nearly fifty years ago.

I THINK it was about 1932 that I had a letter from a woman whose name was strange to me. She was Marion Scott, but as I did not move in musical circles I did not know that she was distinguished in that world. The subject of her letter was strange to me for the same reason. I was therefore filled with surprise and pity when she told me that she was the champion and friend of a young musical genius named Ivor Gurney. This young man had lost his reason in the war and was in a lunatic asylum. He passionately loved my husband's work and was deeply interested in anything to do with him. Indeed Edward Thomas's name—for Ivor Gurney had never met him though they had been near each other at the front in France —evoked in him what one can only call love. She wrote saying that if I could face the ordeal of visiting him, she felt such indirect contact with Edward would mean more to him than we could imagine. So it was arranged that I should go. I met Miss Scott at Victoria Station and I had my hands full of flowers.

On the journey to Dartford she told me about him, how he came of a very humble Gloucestershire family, how he had always been highly sensitive and eccentric and that those fit to judge thought him a musical genius. How his mind—always on the borderline—had quite given way at the front and how he had tried more than once to take his own life.

We arrived at Dartford Asylum which looked like—as indeed it was—a prison. A warder let us in after unlocking a door, and doors were opened and locked behind us as we were ushered into the building. We were walking along a bare corridor when we were met by a tall gaunt dishevelled man clad in pyjamas and dressing gown, to whom Miss Scott introduced me. He gazed with an intense stare into my face and took me silently by the hand. Then I gave him the flowers which he took with the same deeply moving intensity and silence. He then said, 'You are Helen, Edward's wife and Edward is dead.' And I said, 'Yes, let us talk of him.'

So we went into a little cell-like bedroom where the only furniture was a bed and a chair. The window was high and barred and the walls bare and drab. He put the flowers on the bed for there was no vessel to put them in; there was nothing in the room that could in any way be used to do damage with —no pottery or jars or pictures whose broken edge could be used as a weapon.

He remarked on my pretty hat, for it was summer and I had purposely put on my brightest clothes. The gay colours gave him great pleasure. I sat by him on the bed and we talked of Edward and of himself, but I cannot now remember the conversation. But I do remember that though his talk was generally quite sane and lucid, he said suddenly, 'It was wireless that killed Edward', and this idea of the danger of wireless and his fear of it constantly occurred in his talk. 'They are getting at me through wireless.' We spoke of country that he knew and which Edward knew too and he evidently identified Edward with the English countryside, especially that of Gloucestershire.

I learned from the warder that Ivor Gurney refused to go into the grounds of the asylum. It was not his idea of the country at all—the fields, woods, water-meadows and footpaths he loved so well—and he would have nothing to do with that travesty of something sacred to him.

Before we left he took us into a large room in which was a piano and on this he played to us and to the tragic circle of men who sat on hard benches built into the walls of the room. Hopeless and aimless faces gazed vacantly and restless hands fumbled or hung down lifelessly. They gave no sign or sound that they heard the music. The room was quite bare and there was not one beautiful thing for the patients to look at.

We left and I promised to come again.

Ivor Gurney longed more than anything else to go back to his native Gloucestershire, but this was not allowed for fear he should again try to take his own life. I said, 'But surely it would be more humane to let him go there even if it meant no more than one hour of happiness before he killed himself.' But the authorities could not look at it in that way.

The next time I went with Miss Scott I took with me Edward's own well-used ordnance maps of Gloucestershire where he had often walked. This proved to have been a sort of inspiration for Ivor Gurney at once spread them out on his bed and he and I spent the whole time I was there tracing with our fingers the lanes and byways and villages of which Ivor Gurney knew every step and over which Edward had also walked. He spent that hour in revisiting his home, in spotting a village or a track, a hill or a wood and seeing it all in his mind's eye, with flowers and trees, stiles and hedges, a mental vision sharper and more actual for his heightened intensity. He trod, in a way we who were sane could not emulate, the lanes and fields he knew and loved so well, his guide being his finger tracing the way on the map. It was most deeply moving, and I knew that I had hit on an idea that gave him more pleasure than anything else I could have thought of. For he had Edward as companion in this strange perambulation and he was utterly happy, without being over-excited.

This way of using my visits was repeated several times and I became for a while not a visitor from the outside world of war and wireless, but the element which brought Edward back to life for him and the country where they two could wander together.

A REMEMBERED HARVEST

[I have chosen this piece to finish Mother's memories, not because it happens to be the last she wrote, but because it evokes her eager spirit and her love of the earth and of those who work on it and are part of it. —M.T.]

SIXTY YEARS ago we lived for three full years on a farm, Elses Farm, in the Weald of Kent, and looking back over my long life I choose this period as the happiest—the one during which my knowledge of and intimacy with the English country and farming way of life were immensely deepened. So much so that for ever after, even though I had to be alone, in no other element could my spirit and body be satisfied.

There, in that plain but dignified mellowed red brick farmhouse standing vigilant in its own fields, I became familiar with the rhythm of the seasons and the activities which inevitably went with each. It was chiefly a dairy farm and was farmed by our landlord, Mr Killick, who only let us the spacious farm house as he preferred living above his dairy shop in Sevenoaks. We became identified with the great variety of work which went on without haste or noise, done by men who understood and whose fathers had understood the tough Kentish clay and made it fruitful.

The hop garden was on the southern border of the farm, beyond the great oaks of Blooming Meadow in which the house stood, and it was a pleasant walk, just as far as the children, who were babies, could manage. Over the meadow by the hedge, through the gap by the pond, and there you were.

I had watched from the early time of the year the cultivation of the hops, involving a variety of skills, from the ploughing with horses between the 'hills'—the perennial hop plants of which nothing could be seen in winter but the slightly rounded mounds stretching away in symmetrical rows—to the delicate 'twiddling' of the bines when the shoots appeared and had to be trained to the strings which had already been stretched criss-cross from pole to pole. The strings made an intricate design, seeming to envelop the garden in a glowing mist.

But it is the great festival of the year on our farm that I

113

want to recall, for it had a pagan quality, age-old and primitive, which especially appealed to me. The strings, by this time late in August, were covered with the harsh hop bines and their golden pungent fruit hanging in bountiful garlands among the dark leaves. This was the time for the harvesting of the hops—more like flowers than fruit, with petals overlapping. Under the green arches, canvas troughs slung on rough wooden frames were placed in rows some feet apart, but close enough for the pickers to chat and exchange jokes and gossip with each other.

The picking on our farm was done by village women and children: the garden was not large enough for the need of 'east-enders', who emigrated in their thousands to other parts of Kent from Lambeth and Whitechapel to spend six weeks on the Kent clay to replenish their marvellous vitality. For us the only men to give zest to the bawdy jokes which the atmosphere of this harvest evoked, even in the most chapel-minded women, were the tally-men, perhaps six to this small garden. These men had much to do. It was their job to cut, with the razor-edged sickle-shaped knife at the end of a long pole, the bines from the strings and drape these armfuls of hop-laden tendrils over the bar of wood raised above the trough so that the pickers could loosen the tangle and rob its fruit, dropping each hop separately—never in bunches—into the bin.

I was there with my maid, Daisy Turner, and my two children: Bronwen only a baby carried by one of us, and Merfyn, a sturdy boy of four. When the ceremony began (hop-picking had its strict etiquette and procedure) each trough had already been garlanded by its share of bines and beside each waited the women and their families. Until the tally-man blew his horn not a hop might be picked, and in those far-away days law and order entered into every department of life. Especially, I think, was this so in those activities closely related to the earth. Even in the wild prodigality of nature there is a rhythm and order with which the countryman is instinct. So that the heady smell of the hops and the freedom from indoor chores evoked in the women an element of licentiousness and all went as merrily as a marriage bell during those golden revels.

The horn having sounded we fell to our picking and this was done by experienced women, who from babyhood had been trained in this skill, with delicate neatness and swiftness. The hops that fell into the bin had to be clean of any leaf and of each other. It took me a long time to learn how to do this. The hop fruit is a cone of petals, and the skilled picker will manage to detach one from its bunch whole and compact without, as I often did, scattering the fruit in a flurry of petals into the bin. Children sat on little stools or piles of coats with a box or bucket or perhaps a hat between their chubby knees. Their mothers would throw them bunches of hops to pick and when their buckets were full they would proudly add the contents to the mounting mass in the bin.

The tally-man would come round and cry, 'Pick up yer 'ops! Pick up yer 'ops!' Especially with inexperienced pickers and children some hops were dropped on the ground, and each had to be retrieved, for there must be no waste and no untidiness in this harvest. With him the women would bandy words, and always there was a hilarious and pretended enmity between them and this master of ceremonials, and though Daisy would laugh uproariously at some of the bawdiness, it was so new to me I did not understand it at all, but I knew by the quality of the laughter and the look in the eyes of the jokers that the ribaldry was of the dark earth of which I, townbred and innocent, knew nothing.

At noon the horn would sound and we must finish picking the bine we had in hand, for to begin a new one was forbidden. Now the tally-man came with his bushel-basket to measure the hops each picker had in her trough, and with a lovely gesture the women plunged their bare arms deep into their cargo and with a sort of flutter of the hands and fingers raised the heavy load to let the air and space into their packing, so that the precious fruit would go lightly into the tally-man's measure and pile up to the bushel mark more quickly. With what keen eyes they watched his measure, for pay was by the bushel. I think the pay for my pick entered in the tally-man's book was sixpence.

Now with our appetites whetted by the heady hop-impregnated air we sat around our bins for lunch. This consisted of the traditional bottles of cold tea and slabs of baked bread-pudding full of fruit and brown sugar, sticky and extremely satisfying. We sat on the hard clay, enjoying the food and laughing and talking. The children got restive when they had eaten their fill and played hide-and-seek in the still untouched bowers, and the suckled babies were changed and put back in their prams. The women's rough and golden-stained hands were for a moment idle. Looking away down the avenue of green leaves I could glimpse brightly coloured groups of women and children in attitudes of repose and presently a silence would fall under that fruit-laden darkness of leaves and the children would curl up by their mothers and sleep, and the women, unused to idleness, would nod. The tally-men lay flat out on their backs with heads resting on their upraised hands, and there would be no sound but the murmur of insects and distant lowing of cattle.

Such a scene, such a quality of living enriched my spirit for ever.

But the horn blew and quickly each got to her task and the bins were filled and measured again and again until the sun lowered behind the hill and we picked our last hop at the command of the horn.

The tally-men now turned to their last job of moving the long rows of troughs into unravished aisles. Each woman noted her new position for tomorrow, and straggling home with children whimpering with tiredness, she faced the evening's work, cross with the heat, but happy and satisfied having earned perhaps ten shillings. After a fortnight's picking each received her money upon which she depended for the children's winter boots and perhaps a new jacket for her man and for those necessary things the ordinary wages could not stretch to.

'Good night, Mrs Turner.' 'Good night, our Nell.' 'Good night, Mrs Killick.' 'It looks set for fine.'

Helen Noble met and married Edward Thomas and their story is told in Helen Thomas's books *As It Was* and *World Without End*, now published in one volume. The time covered in her memories of childhood and girlhood in the first part of this book, and of her previously published books, is from 11 July 1877, the date of her birth, until 30 January 1917, when Edward left for France. In the following I hope, as the surviving child, to give an idea of Helen's life without Edward. In 1917 Merfyn was seventeen years old, Bronwen fourteen, and I myself rising seven. Apart from the letters and the memoir on D. H. Lawrence, which was written in the late 1920s, all the rest of Helen's work in this book, with the exception of her recollection of conversations at Starwell Farm, was written in the last seven or eight years of her life.

OTFORD

WHEN IN April 1917 the telegraph boy leaned his red bicycle against the fence outside the Nurseryman's cottage on the edge of Epping Forest, Mother and I were sewing. I am sure she knew what the telegram would say, before the knock came at the door. I remember no words or tears, only the white face above me as my coat was put on, and we hurried to the post office, I having to trot to keep up with her quick step. Clutching her hand tightly, I remember looking up once or twice for a companionable glance at me. I waited outside while telegrams were sent to Granny Thomas, Mother's younger sister Mary and to Eleanor Farjeon.

Merfyn and Bronwen were away and mother and I went almost at once to stay with Mary in London, now married to a consulting engineer and with one daughter, Margaret, a year older than Bronwen, who was my particular favourite.

Helen longed to get back to Kent where she and Edward had been happiest, and very soon she heard of a Tudor cottage—Forge House—at Otford, owned by a Mrs Gilchrist Thompson, who generously let it to her at a very small rent. Helen's only income at first was an army pension, later to be supplemented by a small civil list one. Merfyn had enlisted and Bronwen, who went back to Bedales for a short time, was soon in London as a companion to old Mrs Farjeon, mother of Eleanor and Harry, the eldest son, who lived with her. Bertie and Jo Farjeon were married.

I, being much the youngest of the family, was treated like an only child, rather spoiled, and with Mother continually. To be parted from her even for a night had always been agony for me. If for any reason she went out leaving me at home, I listened apprehensively for the beat of her quick firm step. I never forgot the terror of being told by a neighbour that she had 'gone for a soldier'.

While Mother worked hard at organizing her new life and trying to enter into the life of the village, the village street was my playground. The blacksmith, Mr Hartnup, worked in his forge next door and I spent hours watching him shoe the great farm-horses, or fit iron rims to the cartwheels. He made the boys iron hoops with iron hooks to guide them, while the girls bowled wooden ones. I envied the boys their hoops and the sparks that flew from the hook when they were bowled down the street.

In summer the water-cart would amble up the road on hot dusty days, pulled by an old pony. It was a metal cylinder on a two-wheeled frame and water sprayed out from it in arching jets to settle the dust. I learned to run under the spray with the village children, until one of the boys called out 'Whip behind, Mister', and the man leading the horse would flick his whip at us, making the girls squeal. There was Darkie Day, too, a swarthy, surly man with thick black beard and unkempt hair under his shapeless hat, who came round with his flat-bottomed cart with oil-cans clanking round it, kettles he had mended, faggots of peasticks and a great drum of paraffin with its tap overhanging the tail of the cart. The more daring boys would run behind, cling on to the tail-board and have a few yards' ride, their metal-tipped boots scuffing the road and sparking, while the less brave called out, 'Darkie darkie Day', at a safe distance, ready to run off if he should turn round with his whip.

Charlie Browning, the milkman, came every day with shining brass-bound churns and a rail on the pony-drawn float hung with bright tin measures on hooked brass handles. Jugs covered with saucers were left outside the back door and I delighted to watch Charlie dip into the large churn filled with frothy milk with the pint measure, pouring it deftly into the jug and always a generous extra dip for good measure.

The butcher had a smart, high-wheeled trap, the joints of meat in scrubbed flat wicker baskets behind him. The baker's van, horse-drawn of course, had an arched canvas cover and he came to the back door with a huge wicker basket covered with a white cloth, its handle, thicker than his wrist, over his shoulder. He would slide the basket down his arm and you chose the hot crisp loaves, cottage or coburg, tin or sandwich.

There were three pubs: The Horns, kept by Mr Lintott; The Woodman; and The Bull. Occasionally open char-a-bancs loaded with singing thirsty men on a works outing pulled up at The Bull. The village pond stood at the top of the village, with the green on three sides, edged with fine Georgian houses —the Macleans, the Wellbands, the Brownings. The pond had a stone arch over a drinking fountain with a thick tin cup on a chain, a horse trough below. Into the arch were set chunks of blue and green glass, which I regarded as jewels and often tried to pry off with a broken knife. The church stood at the top end, near the green, with a slouching sideways table tomb in the churchyard from which, it was said, you could hear the devil speak if you ran round it three times counterclockwise. I was enchanted by the white icing-sugar doves and lilies under glass domes lying on many of the graves. There was a Wesleyan chapel at the other end, where the Darenth flowed through an orchard of quinces.

Once a week there was a bus into Sevenoaks, when Mother and I would go shopping. Mother enjoyed listening to the gossip at the bus-stop by the pond. She was particularly delighted at a remark about the vicar's wife who waited apart from the gossiping group—'What a bitch the woman is—and *look* at the hang of her coat!' And another time, when Bronwen, an occasional visitor from London, had gone to a village fancy dress dance in a very attractive *pierette* costume—'And my dear, the *whole* thing was supported by two shoulder-straps!'

If the roads were slippery or the bus particularly full—it was an open-topped double-decker—the more able of us had to get out and walk up the hill into the centre of Sevenoaks, while the conductor walked behind with a great wedge-shaped block of wood with a handle, ready to put under the back wheels in case of need.

I think Mother must have been a puzzle to the village and regarded as rather bohemian. There were two or three young war-widows who wore deep mourning, the bereaved mothers wearing the nun-like black headdress of those days; but mother had never worn mourning, and dressed in warm bright colours, rust, yellow and green, and behaved in an unconventional way, often bringing her sewing to the step of our front door on the village street and hobnobbing with the villagers, while allowing me to play in the road. On summer nights, with the gramophone on the doorstep, I danced in the dusty road to my dark shadow.

In Otford lived Mrs Thorndike, the mother of Sybil and Russell, and Helen with her love of the theatre soon got to know the family. Mrs Thorndike, with her pile of corn-coloured hair, was an elaborately dressed lady, her low-cut dresses revealing a much-powdered bosom on which lay a large crucifix encrusted with amethysts. She often looked in for a cup of tea on her way to the station to meet friends, and later on, Helen went for long walks to Kemsing or Westerham with Sybil and Russell. Helen also made friends with the actor Alan Anderson and his wife. On the top floor of their house was a pigeon loft, said once to have been used when important ecclesiastical messages were sent from Wolsey's Otford palace to Canterbury.

I remember other interesting characters: a lady who lived in one of the large Georgian houses on the village green, who kept several Pekinese dogs known as 'the children'. In the small hours of one morning she telephoned to ask if Mother had any champagne, as one of 'the children' was ill. Mother replied sleepily and to the old lady's annoyance, 'Oh dear, I thought your grandchildren had gone back to school.' There was a cinema proprietor, Mr Underwood, who drove through the village to the station every morning in an open landau, with silk hat, fat cigar and a large dahlia in his buttonhole.

The girls of the village, my playmates in the quiet street at hopscotch, skipping, hoops and 'One two three allairy, I saw Sister Mary, sitting on a wool-allairy, kissing Tommy Atkins' while bouncing a ball, or joining in the more daring ball-game of Tishy-toshy against a wall—the girls deserve a place for themselves. Di Steers, Topsy Wellstead and Topsy Booker, Bell Kemp, Kitty Fordham, Vi, Lily and Ivy Booker, three sisters—'Our dad said with Lily and Vi we'll have a bit of greenery and call the little 'un Ivy'—dressed in the week in dark dresses and pinafores, black stockings and button boots —the boys wore lace-ups with blakeys in the soles and iron tipped heels, making sparks fly as they clobbered down the rough roads. Some of the girls wore their long hair loose with the two side bits drawn back and plaited with a bow on the end, but mostly—like Topsy Wellstead's—in twenty or more thin tight plaits, turned up at the ends with bits of tightly knotted rag, the plaits bobbing and flying as they skipped and jumped. Only on Sunday was the full glory seen. On that day, before chapel, Mum undid the plaits and brushed

122

out the hair so that it crimped and fluffed and stood out in a pre-Raphaelite frizz, tied with long white ribbons to match the Sunday pinafore of *broderie anglaise*, starched and goffered at neck and bottom frill, lace-edged drawers showing below best frock, and black stockings with no holes and best boots with no buttons missing. One of them, Glad, I think it was, was pale and plump, unable to skip and bowl hoops, as her leg had been taken off above the knee and she wore a wooden peg leg strapped to her thigh; there was a particular smell of warm greasy leather about her, cloying and sweetish. One girl had her hair in tight curl-rags all over her head in the week and her mother, on Sundays, undid the curl-rags and brushed each long curl round a hoop-stick so that she had golden ringlets, like Mary Pickford, hanging stiffly down her back.

I envied this Sunday splendour of ringlets and frizz, for my hair was cut short with a fringe, straight and unresponsive. Sometimes, when my playmates were at the village school, with the disintegrating snakes preserved in jamjars in the high windows, I collected curly shavings from our neighbour's workshop. He made 'antique' furniture and had a special gadget for drilling woodworm holes in the table legs for good measure. I would fix the blond corkscrew shavings under my hat, tossing them over my shoulder with the nonchalant movement I so much admired.

There was a girl of about fourteen who lived with her mother in a very dark little villa on the green, closely guarded with thick dusty laurels—Olive Gidney. She never went to school, nor was she ever seen except with her mother, Mrs Gidney, who gave piano lessons. They were always very genteelly dressed, with hats and gloves, never speaking to anyone except in the shops, and then in whispers. Olive Gidney had two long snake-like plaits, plaited to the tiniest possible, with little black tidy bows on the end, which reached to her knees. We were in awe of pale Olive because Mrs Gidney had once put it about the village that if Olive had her long hair cut she would die, as all her strength, like Samson's, was in her hair. The wiser women of the village, judging Olive by her unhealthy pallor and prim gait, thought otherwise and that if Mrs Gidney had any sense she would cut the poor girl's hair off and she would be like anyone else.

The boys, even if they were the girls' brothers, were never spoken to or played with. They went birds'-nesting or frog-hunting. I remember running in to Mother in anguish about what the boys were doing to the frogs in the ditch, and how she came hurrying out with her quick step, trouncing them saying, 'You're worse than Germans,' when they slunk away and hid. They had top-whips made of a leather bootlace tied to a copper stick and their tops were called window-breakers and would leap into the air in a great arc and continue spinning to be whipped up again. Often the boys had shorn heads with white bald patches on their scalps, a sign of ring-worm. The girls didn't seem to suffer from this humiliating complaint, possibly because the boys did more about the farms, helping dad with the cows, and were more subject to catching it. The girls would occasionally 'call after' the boys, at a safe distance. There was one huge simple fellow called Charlie Bingham of whom we were all very scared, and if he was in a group of boys we'd call 'Wotcher Binger-Bonger' which made him turn round and pretend to run at us, when we would turn tail squealing.

This was during the last year of the war, when Mother was doing her utmost to settle down to village life alone, to making a garden, to eking out the small pension to feed and clothe herself, Bronwen and me and to make some sort of life for us. I remember her reaction to factory-made jam being sweetened with glucose, and being proud that she had never had to buy the unwholesome stuff, but made her own preserves by scrimping and scraping with her sugar ration. I was left very much to my own devices, another reason I daresay for the gentry of the village not being more hospi-table and friendly. I had occasional lessons with a pretty child whose father was away at the front, taught by her mother's housekeeper, a fearsome old lady who some thought to be the attractive Mrs Seagrim's mother. The lessons came to an end when I developed scabies after Captain Seagrim had been home on short leave, and had to have sulphur baths and be plastered in yellow ointment to get rid of the burrowing parasites.

Helen joined the Women's Institute in its early years. The

ladies of the village paid her formal calls, which Mother returned, with the leaving of cards. But these visits seldom led to warm friendships. She took me to the village 'Socials', where I would sometimes contribute a dance to the programme of comic songs, dramatic recitations, hilarious sketches and sentimental duets, 'Oh that we two were maying' accompanied by Miss Violet Underwood on an upright piano with one or two dud notes.

The best times were those evenings, when I had Mother entirely to myself and while I sat sewing she read aloud to me, *David Copperfield, The Purple Land, Jackanapes, The Cuckoo Clock, Treasure Island*, and a particular favourite of mine called *Down the Snow Stairs*, a very moral and rather frightening story which Mother had found in a Sevenoaks bookshop and bought secondhand, remembering it from her own childhood. And after my bath, sitting by the great open fireplace, eating my bread and milk supper very slowly, she sang songs Edward had taught her, 'All round my hat', 'I sowed the seeds of love', 'Little Sir William', 'Barbara Allen'— I loved the sad ones especially.

Then came the maroons and the bonfires and the war was over.

Weekends often brought visitors: Merfyn and Bronwen and their friends, uncles, aunts and cousins. Uncle Ernest Thomas, a commercial artist, came with Florrie his wife and Dick, their son a little younger than I, to live in Otford. Bronwen earned a bit of pocket money sitting to him in various sporting outfits which we later saw in shop windows advertising C. B. Corsets; she was 'The C. B. Girl'. And I was his model once for a cod-liver oil advertisement. They lived in a turning up from The Woodman, which had been bombed by a zeppelin and was regarded as a slum by the more genteel inhabitants.

I was now going to a day-school kept by two French ladies in Sevenoaks. Helen was filling her days with theatre going, having piano lessons in London—I remember her seeing Sybil Thorndike in *St Joan* and going to a series of Grand Guignol plays in which Franklin Dyall acted—an old friend of hers and Edward's in their young days. At weekends Merfyn came down from London on his Triumph motorbike on which I was sometimes privileged to ride on the carrier, my legs sticking out in a V-shape to avoid getting caught in the rear wheel.

The following letter, to Janet Hooton, gives an idea of Helen's life at about this time.

29 January 1920   Forge House
                                                        Otford
My dear Janet,
   Don't ask me to explain why I've not written to you all this time, for I couldn't tell you—a mix up of reasons and un-reasons. Don't ask me why at midnight tonight I suddenly think I will write to you for I don't know. Three years ago today Edward went away from me. The snow was deep on the ground and he soon disappeared in a thick fog, and we coo-eed to each other until we could not hear any more, and I was left alone knowing I would never see him never hear him never hold him in my arms again. Tonight I'm thinking of all our life together, and I'm thinking of my life during those three years. Our life together was a restless sea, tide in tide out, calm and storm, despair and ecstasy; never still, never easy, but always vivid and moving wave upon wave a wide deep glorious sea, our life was terrible and glorious but always life. And I'm thinking of my life these three years. And again it has been like a sea, calm and cruel, happy and despairing, just the same as always but without a harbour without an anchorage, and I have been tired to death of this tossing to and fro on to this beach and that, on to that rock and that. For life for me cannot be otherwise until that new life comes to me and I am gathered into my anchorage and live and yet am calm.
   Merfyn is out of the army back at his engineering. He is twenty and quiet and affectionate and reserved and loyal. He has made for himself standards and ideals crude I daresay but to those he sticks. He is my comfort for he loves me and it's lovely to have a big son whose instinct is to protect and cherish.
   Bronwen is seventeen and very beautiful. She is the gayest, the brightest, the sweetest thing you can think of. She's very frivolous and irresponsible and extravagant. Her love is all on

126

the surface at least a good deal of it is. She has admirers wherever she goes and treats them very disdainfully, tho' she could not be without them. She loves clothes and the theatre and ragtime and above all dancing. Merfyn adores her and she him. She's irresistible. Ernest Thomas [Edward's next brother] has just painted a very lovely portrait of her. She's living with Mary in London and learning dress designing at the L.C.C. school in Hammersmith. She and Merfyn and Margaret Valon are all coming home for the weekend to a dance. We have a gramophone with all the newest musical comedy songs and jazz bands.

Myfanwy is nine. Tall and slim and would be lovely but for her specs. She is very clever and amusing and has all Edward's wonderful power of observation only directed to people. She misses nothing and is wonderfully right. She reads a very great deal and plays with dolls. She loves acting and dancing and loves people. She is a loyal friend like Edward and her idol is me. I am for her perfect, her adoration is almost painful for it is so sensitive. Her brain is like Edward's and her search for truth is like his. She is a wonderful mimic and terribly acquisitive. She's never been punished and she and I understand each other perfectly. She goes to school and is not at all brilliant but she has a wonderful intellect and character.

I, I am told am no older than ever I was. My hair is very grey nevertheless. I am very rich in all that matters. Love and friends and children and health and capacity for life. My life is full of interest—people and books and thoughts and emotions and work. I walk a lot on the downs and was in Scotland in the summer climbing mountains and bathing in mountain streams and exploring glens. I get to the South Downs whenever I can. I have walked the whole length several times of late. I love it. I am writing too of my life with Edward from our meeting. Eleanor says it is good but I'm not sure. I do it because I like it and it comforts me.

Today I was reading *The Icknield Way* and the dedication [To Harry Hooton]. I remember so much that we all did together. Isn't life strange? How are your girls and you two. You are one of those blest women whose beloved is with you. I always want to speak with mine and listen to him and look at him and hold him tight in my arms so that he can never leave me again. When I see Merfyn and Bronwen dancing together I want to say to him, 'Look at your lovely children, they are ours those two young things, we made them out of our love, isn't it glorious'. And he would be cross with me for such foolishness and I would kiss him for his crossness and he would like my kiss and be still crosser. And I would understand and he would know all I know. I often dream like that. You see how I talk to myself. You'll think me selfish and self centred, but I'm not really. I'm very much the same   Helen.

*   *   *

Bronwen became engaged to Geoffrey Page, brother of Kate, her contemporary at Bedales. Kate was married to Hubert Foss, a young musician, living at the next but one village of Eynsford. Bronwen by then was helping Kate with her two little girls. On Sundays, Kate and Hubert with a party of musicians, would walk over from Eynsford: Moeran, Philip Heseltine—later to call himself Peter Warlock—(he set Bronwen's poem by Edward, 'If I should ever by chance grow rich . . .', to music for her; it was lost in one of her many moves), Van Dieren, John Goss the singer and sometimes Francis Meynell, the founder of the Nonesuch Press.

The men, with Merfyn and Uncle Ernest, would play a wild game of rounders, have a drink at The Bull and then drift in to Forge House for tea and rejoin the girls who had come with them but funked the rounders. I recall my admiration of such self-assurance when one of these girls, Jessica, dark and pale, her hair elaborately dressed in Grecian coils and ringlets, looked into a glass and drawled, 'My God, how plain I am today—but then one can't always live up to one's reputation!'

It was about this time that I started school at Tonbridge, living with my Aunt Mary and Uncle Arthur and my beloved cousin Margaret, returning to Mother at Otford most weekends. I think she had already begun secretly to write her memories of Edward, at the suggestion of a friend, as a means of easing the intolerable loss and grief and loneliness of

128

spirit. When I came home to Otford, there was a restlessness in the house. It now seemed to be always full of noisy people, often quarelling, with crying children and Mother having to give up her room and sleep on a couch downstairs. Kate and Hubert and their friends, and mother distractedly providing meals at all hours. When I got back one Friday evening, after staying at Tonbridge for several weekends, I saw that straw was strewn on the village street outside our house. Mother was desperately ill.

HAMPSTEAD

HELEN'S doctor told her she should go and live in London nearer friends, where she could have more distractions. So, when she was a bit stronger she let Forge House to Kate and Hubert and took furnished lodgings in Hampstead in a house belonging to C. E. M. Joad. From there she visited several specialists, none of whom seemed to be able to diagnose her condition, which caused attacks of excruciating pain. In the end it was a Dr Sorapure, half Irish, half Portuguese, and not on the medical register, who decided that it was a case of delayed shock, and set about curing her. He came every day to Joad's house to give her treatment, which was later continued less frequently by one of his trained nurses.

I came up to stay with Mother occasionally from Tonbridge, and I remember Joad taking me to see a performance of *The Rose and the Ring* and taking me behind afterwards to meet his friend Miles Malleson.

The house next door to Joad's—it is a terrace of six Victorian houses in the Vale of Health—had been empty for some years and was on the verge of becoming derelict. Some of the windows were boarded up, and one or two of the stone steps leading up to the front door were broken and crumbling. Very reluctantly Helen gave up the tenancy of Forge House and bought the leasehold of the Hampstead one. She lived in part of the house; Bronwen and Geoffrey Page, now married, rented two rooms and there was a lodger on the top floor, their rents helping to pay the heavier expenses of living in London.

Helen's first volume of autobiography, *As it Was*, was published in 1926 under the initials H. T. and for several weeks its sales rivalled those of Margaret Kennedy's best-selling novel *The Constant Nymph*. Five years later the sequel, *World Without End* was published and once again it was very well received. For a time Helen became quite a celebrity. There was a review of her book broadcast by Vita Sackville-West; at that time I was a typist at the BBC in Savoy Hill, and I remember our supervisor in tears when she checked the script with me. We were invited to dine with the Harold Nicolsons at Long Barn near Sevenoaks. When we arrived their two sons, handsome and elegant boys of about eight and eleven, told us that their parents were having baths after a long walk. They chatted to us with ease and confidence and asked us where we had parked our car, as they had not been able to find it. We didn't come by car, we told them. 'Oh, you came by plane then—where *is* it?' said the younger boy with great interest and a hint of excitement. We had to admit that we had walked from Sevenoaks, where we were staying.

Living at the first of the six Victorian villas was John Middleton Murry and his enchanting second wife Violet, who looked, we agreed, great theatre-goers as we were, exactly like the young Jessie Matthews, then making her debut in the Charlot Revues at the Prince of Wales Theatre. They had two very small children, and Violet, who was completely undomesticated, often came round to Helen for advice about cooking or the babies. She would burst into tears like a child and as quickly, when Jack Murry had found a hankie to dry her cheeks, would be smiling again.

Helen had a mischievous sense of fun and could keep a completely straight face to bring off a piece of nonsense. At one time the top floor was let to a serious-minded young woman named Molly. Usually she was shy and withdrawn, so it was with some surprise and pleasure that Helen and Bronwen were invited upstairs to her flat to have coffee one evening. It gradually transpired that Molly wanted to try out a planchette and needed the help of two others. Never having seen one of these boards in operation, Helen and Bronwen willingly consented. The planchette was put on the card table, an upsidedown wineglass placed in the centre and each of the three laid a finger on the bottom rim. Their host asked the planchette several questions and the wineglass moved hesitantly towards various letters but spelt out nothing sensible. Helen was very shrewd and she soon judged by the questions Molly was asking so eagerly that she wanted to get in touch with an absent gentleman friend whom Helen had occasionally seen at the front door. The wine glass continued to haver and hover and Helen, the time getting on, was becoming bored. So with a little gentle pressure on the rim she guided the glass to spell out relevant answers. 'Are you *there*, William?' Molly would ask anxiously. The glass suddenly obliged with 'Yes!' Molly perked up and proceeded to ask William more questions which were answered satisfactorily. Helen could see the time by her watch on the wrist above the wineglass and with a brilliant stroke of memory made the glass spell out a fond goodnight, using the pet-name which she recalled the gentleman friend having used one day when he greeted Molly at the front door. And so the session ended and everyone went to bed happy, Helen looking as innocent as an April morning, Molly flushed and satisfied and Bronwen mystified.

Helen was by now completely recovered and through the success of her books had at last confidence in herself. She enjoyed discussion and laughter. She went to the theatre a great deal—I remember our delight and enchantment at seeing La Compagnie de Quinze giving a performance of *Noé*, and later on when she saw the same company doing Shakespeare's *Rape of Lucrece* at the house of Lady Cunard, Helen's disgust at the behaviour of the society audience. She wrote me a fine letter describing the women in their white satin gowns, with their exquisitely sun-tanned arms and shoulders, showing their diamonds to advantage, bundling up their arctic fox furs to make a cushion on the little gilt chairs; how the quartet who were performing one of Helen's favourite Mozart pieces were stopped suddenly in the middle of their performance because a draught was causing the music to fall off the stands, and how when the leader asked if the door could be closed, the hostess snatched up the music stands and cleared the stage. The delicate and sensitive performance of *Lucrece* was hardly noticed—there was waving, whispering, fluttering of false eyelashes and ostrich feather fans, and remarks from some of the handsome young guardsmen like, 'Rather near the knuckle, what?' Helen was hot with shame at being associated with such an ill-mannered and insensitive crowd, and would not stay with Eleanor, whose guest she was, to join the champagne supper afterwards, but stalked out and got a taxi home.

Helen began to recall the fun Edward and she had had—how the only time they had been to the cinema or Picture Palace as it was then called, at Petersfield, during the big picture the screen had suddenly turned a flickering lurid red and the caption read 'The Baron, flushed with wine, calls for Mary', which made them laugh so much they had to go out, and I think that was their first and last visit. How when Arthur and Ivy Ransome were secretly married at a registry office where Edward and Helen were witnesses, they had a champagne supper and then took the stage box at a music hall. Arthur Ransome was very merry and when Vesta Victoria came on and began to sing, 'And now I have to call him Father', she caught his eye and began to laugh herself; several times she tried to begin her song again but Arthur's laughter was so infectious that she was convulsed with giggles. So much so that the manager came into the box and said that if the gentleman could not control himself, he would have to go out. Sitting on the edge of the box, Vesta Victoria at last sang her song. Arthur Ransome insisted on going round to the stage door and when he met the singer he gave her a hearty kiss. Ivy, the new bride, was furious and demanded that he washed his mouth out with carbolic before the honeymoon began.

Helen's circle of friends had been widening as she renewed old friendships with John and Phyllis Richardson whom she had met in the early Otford days, and made new ones, particularly Alan Thomas, who was now literary editor of *The Listener* and the author of a number of novels and detective stories, and his wife, Elsa. She also got to know Franklyn Lushington and his wife Bridget. Franklyn had been Edward's commanding officer in France. He was about twenty years younger than Edward, straight from Woolwich, and after the war had published a book of his experiences under the pseudonym of Mark Severn in which there was a keen thumbnail sketch of Edward as a soldier. The Lushingtons and Helen became close friends and Helen often went to see them at their pretty Tudor cottage near Tenterden.

Also living in Hampstead at that time was an old friend of Helen and Edward, Ian MacAlister, then Secretary of the Royal Institute of British Architects. Edward had first met 'Mac' at Oxford, and Bronwen had been a bridesmaid at his wedding. He and his wife Dorothy lived in Well Walk and Mac and two or three of their large family of children would walk over the Heath to see us on Sunday mornings.

Helen's new found self-confidence developed her splendid gift of discussion and criticism. She enjoyed expressing her own anger against and condemnation of hypocrisy, pretentiousness and cruelty. She vehemently defended her heroes—Nelson, Dickens, Keats and Shakespeare. She loved to air her prejudices, often quite unreasonably. One of these was Bernard Shaw. To her he lacked that essential quality which she loved above all others: warmth. She had seen only one or two of his plays, but she *knew* she would dislike them, his characters were bloodless—all intellect and no heart.

On the other hand she was disgusted with those who insisted on going against Hardy's wishes to be buried in Stinsford churchyard and was horrified at the idea of taking his heart from his body as a kind of conciliatory act. She wrote an impassioned letter of protest to one of the literary periodicals and to ease her feelings wrote these verses:

I met a ghost who wandered
About his Abbey tomb
Who sadly walked and pondered
And whispered to the gloom—

'What strange bed have they made me
Why cooped within these stones
Why exiled have they laid me
Why cindered are my bones?

'I miss my bride beside me
Who gave my heart its flame
My heart that beat inside me
Misses its ribben frame.

'Great men are here around me
No kindred can I claim
I would the earth were round me
And I without this frame

'Lay in my native village
Prone in the earth which knew
The season's tilth and tillage
And the sea birds' mew.

134

'Bone of my bone that earth there
Flesh of my flesh its folk
Trod I those roads from my birth there
Bearing life's galling yoke:

'Asking not fame, but rest.
To journey's end now have I come
Left by the fates in their jest
Ghost without heart without home.'

She defended Epstein's controversial sculpture 'Genesis' vehemently. To her it was a moving work, close to the earth and to truth. She went to see it many times and had many arguments with those who criticized it as obscene or coarse. She was horrified when it was exhibited some years later in an Oxford Street funfair where you paid an extra half-crown to see it, in company with blaring music, suggestive posters, dirty postcards and cheap souvenirs of London.

Her books brought Helen a great many letters from people unknown to her. Several of them became regular visitors or correspondents. It had gradually become known who she was and who the hero of the books was: the sale of Edward's poems rose steadily. Two young men, art students in London, became Helen's friends through her books. She went to stay at the home of one of them, Robin Tanner, at Chippenham in Wiltshire. It was a lively household full of young people, presided over by the warm-hearted and hospitable 'Mother' Tanner. Helen took them on walks around Marlborough and Swindon which she remembered from the time when Edward was preparing the life of Richard Jefferies. To her pride and delight Helen led them unfalteringly to a mediaeval manor at Upper Upham which she and Edward had discovered in a derelict state. They had even contemplated renting it to live in, with its minstrel's gallery and iron cooking pots and roasting jacks, though there was no water. It had now been restored and was lived in. The other young man, Cyril Rice, Robin's friend at the Art School, was engaged to Robin's sister Grace. These carefree times with the eager and unaffected Tanner family made Helen long once again to live in the country, and they found her an eighteenth-century stone-built and stone-tiled farmhouse between Biddestone and Chippenham. The friendly farmer Harold Tucker and his wife Adeline agreed to let half of the house to Helen.

So gradually Helen furnished her half, with some bits from Hampstead and the Caledonian Market, and with odds and ends she bought at local markets and auctions. She sold the Hampstead house to her London maid, Nellie, and her husband, and by the mid-thirties had settled again in the country.

STARWELL FARM

FOR NEARLY twenty years Helen lived a full rich life at Starwell Farm. She went for long walks, finding many rare wild flowers, sometimes alone, often with her young friends; there were midnight expeditions to copses to hear the nightingales; she trundled her wheelbarrow over the fields to gather firewood. When the great ash was struck by lightning over on the Bank and white bone-like splinters were scattered all over the field, what a to-ing and fro-ing there was! Adeline and Harold Tucker took her in their Austin Seven to see villages and churches farther afield. She entered into every aspect of country life with her vigorous spirit: getting her water from the pump outside the back door; heating her irons upturned by the bars of the kitchen range; keeping her paraffin lamps trimmed and filled; going out at dawn to gather mushrooms for the Tuckers to take to Bath market. She was pleased when the roadman, who kept the hedges and banks trimmed, leaving the elegant plants of soapwort and the witchy henbane uncut, saw her walking towards him, her hands full of flowers from the hedgebanks, and remarked admiringly, 'There be you again, sprack as a daisy!' Her green fingers kept her garden a place of scents and colours all year round.

She loved learning about crafts and farming from Harold Tucker and wrote down two conversations she had with him at Starwell.

*　　　*　　　*

'What are you doing, Harold? You sound so happy singing over your work.'

'Come here, Helen, and I'll show you. I'm doing a job that I love doing, and the same tune comes to me every time I do it. Look at this piece of elm.'

'Why, it's a round, Harold. What's it for?'

'I'll tell you in a minute, though you'll laugh. But just look at it, for it's as good a piece of elm as ever I saw. Now compare this round of oak, and this of elm. Which would you choose?'

'Well, both are lovely; the oak is so pretty with its grain as if it were woven into the wood like the satiny damask pattern in fine linen.'

'That pattern is called the *clash* in oak, and I like it too; but it looks to me more like a dappled sky with little dabs of clouds all in a flock. What do you say, Helen? Then there's this elm, and that's my wood—I'll tell you why: the grain goes in such great shapes, and it seems to me as if in the wood you see the very tree itself, the branches going this way and that; and these seem to me to be the great arteries of the tree, up which the sap rushes; and it does rush, Helen, like a full stream—where it is all marked out in the wood in great branch-like patterns. D'you see? I love elm, Helen; it's so strong and living—and yet look how smooth I've got it. Put your hand over it and feel it; you can't feel any grain at all, can you? That's what I was doing when you came along, just gently planing it with this plane, which is what I call my dainty daisy; for she's a real beauty—light on her feet, as you might say, and steady and strong. She's a rare one. I know her and she knows me. She wouldn't be handled by anyone else, and I wouldn't expect it of her. Look at the beech she's made of: a perfect bit of wood for the purpose—smooth as the back of a starling, and as hard as steel. It wouldn't scratch a piece of satin or ivory. It gives the very last finishing touch. We know each other, this plane and I. She knows I won't use her ill, and I know she'll do her job. It fits into my hand: see —like this, and we both understand how to go along together.

'This round is for a table, Helen, to stand by the fire; for I'm going to study in the winter some of the things you've been talking to me about; and I'm going to put my books on it, and it's going to have another, smaller round under it for more books. I want to follow up hints you've dropped of things I'd never thought of before and things that W.E.A. chap was telling us.'

'How good your tools look, Harold: all polished by use and the steel so bright and sharp.'

'They're good tools, though I say it, and they know I'll not use them for any but their lawful jobs. Mostly I re-shape the handles a bit. I flatten them, because my palms are rather flat, and shorten them for my stubby fingers. That's why I dare say they look funny; but for me that's right, because I'm funny too. If I see a good tool in a shop—good shape, good wood, good steel, well fitted and finished, I'm bound to buy it. I like to feel the balance; for if that's right, it's a good start. Then my hand can guide the job, and the tool can do it. If the tool's right for your hand in shape and balance, then your hand and tool become married, as you might say, and it's a love match, sure enough.

'Look at that axe haft: soon I'll get the blade for it, and then the elms will have to look out—for this axe is going to have such a powerful swing, and such an easy running hold, and such a weight and balance, and such a smooth cut, I'll be hard put to it to keep my hands off it. I've seasoned that piece of ash for three years, and it's sound and hardy—and yet with a spring in it. Look how the grain gives the shape for the shaft in that curve, Helen. That's strong, that is, and light, and springy. There'll be no fear with that—the steel head and the ash handle will be just one, working together. No quarrelling. The ash for swing, the steel to cut, and the hands to hold—firm yet light. A good axe that'll be when I've done with it; and I wish I could be sure of swinging it as true as it's made.

'To see some people using tools drives me mad. Push, jamb, scrape and bang, with no thought at all for the ways of the tools. A poor tool doesn't do such bad work in good hands, as a good tool does in bad. I've seen beautiful tools destroyed by bad use. I hate it. Look at this great plane—like a heavy bull to my little daisy. He's a bugger if he's not used right; and I've seen cruel injury done to timber by this plane. He's got a temper; but he trusts me, and I him; so we get on smoothly.

'Look at this little bradall—all worn down. I made it years ago of a bit of right-looking ash I found. That's the shaped handle I like: dumpy like my hand.'

So, leaving the workshop with its saws of all sizes hanging on nails, and its vices and hammers and boxes of nails, and drawers of a thousand oddments which will all come in handy; and the planes in a row, in their sizes, and the fascinating ratchet screwdrivers, and the chisels; and the shavings and sawdust and spiders' webs, we come out from its gloom into the sunlit farmyard and separate.

'Why do you look so glum at the winter oats, Harold? Aren't they doing well? They look all right to me.'

'Well, Helen, I'm not so sure. They want rain, like everything else, and I'm thinking if I shall put the sheep in them and let them nibble them down and put new strength into the roots, and trust to luck the rain comes.'

'What a strange idea. I've never seen that done.'

'It's an old idea, and a good one on some land, and I think I'll do it. The dunging too is good, and this land could do with it. I'll get Nipper on the job, it'll be a lesson for the pup, and for Nip too; for old Nip for all his age is the best dog I've ever had.

'It's a funny thing, Helen, that on this land it's a race between winter sown oats and spring sown oats and barley—which will be ready first. The barley generally wins, though you never get very heavy barley crops here. Last year it was the oats, and that clover over there—you know, the red clover which made such a show. I sow that with the oats, and when the oats are harvested the clover grows and flowers and Adeline's bees come to it in regular routes like aeroplanes; and then I reap it and thresh it for the seed, which is worth a lot these days. But—whether or no—I like it for the bees and the smell. The colour too cheers up the stubble. I'll always have an acre or two of clover.'

'Which crop is your heart most set on, Harold?'

'Well, perhaps the wheat. They're all useful; but there's something about wheat—so heavy and tall; such a colour and such a sound as takes my fancy.

'Now that thirty acres was a poor bit of land: only good enough for sheep, I thought; but when I saw farmer Hinds plough up the next field to it—just such another poor plot—and when I saw the crop of wheat he got off a bit of land no better than mine, I thought to myself, "I'll not be beaten by him!" So I ploughed and sowed, and I had the crop of my life. Such straw—six feet tall and more. I was lost in it. And where there's tall strong straw, there's a good ear. Well, what with the weight of it—fifty bushels an acre for these parts is a heavy harvest—and the strength of it, and the colour of it, well, I said to myself, "I'll save a sheaf for the harvest festival." And so I did. I was that pleased about it!'

'I wish we had the old sort of harvest on this farm, Harold. The combine has spoilt it all. No lovely patterns of stooks; no loading the wagons—no fun at all.'

'That's all very well, Helen; but it's work, and hard work. Men won't do it, and farmers won't pay for it, and the weather oftentimes won't hold for it. So the combine does the whole job and the wheat is reaped and threshed and stored in as many days as it used to take weeks. I'll take you to a farm not far from here, where they do everything in the old way. You'll love it, and I do too. He stacks his wheat in great round stacks on the old stone staddles and the thatch on them is as good as on many a cottage; and the last one to go up is the King stack—and he is crowned with a great straw crown, which one of his old chaps can still make. His rick yard is a sight—and all's done like that. But he's got money behind him, and he owns his land, and has done for hundreds of years; and he won't have a tractor on the place. My father liked that too, though he was a poor man, and the poorer for drink. But drink or no, he could plough with a team for hours, and won the championship year after year. He loved horses as I love tools, and his furrow was like the shaft of a prong, and the slice fell over like the crest of a wave. And all round the field he'd plough so many furrows, to neaten it off like a piece of needlework. It looked good, I can tell you.

'But work! My father was like a bull for strength, and he expected the same of all on the farm, men and women. He planted an orchard of two hundred and fifty trees on rough stony ground himself, without help; and where a dozen men today would take three months to do it, he did it alone in the same time. That was when he was sober; but when he was drunk, he'd drink for weeks and curse all. But the trees flourish to this day; for those roots were properly placed, and that ground properly prepared. You can't get men to work like that now, Helen. But it seems to me it was a good life—plenty of work, good food, and a houseful of men in the evenings by the kitchen fire.

'A job I like is hedging. I like laying a hedge and getting it

141

neat at the sides and on top, pleaching they call it, with the look of a lattice. I leave the sapling elms and the hollies to grow, and I never cut down crab trees—for that's a blossom I love.

'A good laid hedge will last years, and look well, and keep the cattle in, especially if you encourage the thorns; and we've got a lot of buckthorn—which makes the best fence for cows. But sheep are the worst. They break through anything. They never seem satisfied, but are for ever on the wander.

'It's poor land, I know; and yet it can't be so bad, for elms love good land, and you couldn't see finer elms than ours anywhere. Elms and ash—these are our trees, and after all you couldn't ask for better, whether for timber or firing.

'But it's not like Devon with its rich grass lands and heavy crops. But if I had my way, I'd have a first class herd of cows —Ayrshires I like—they're fine to look at and good milkers. I'd like some like the squire's—white faces and curved horns: clean, sound, lovely beasts. But it all takes money, Helen. But—though I know you laugh at me for saying it—it'll all come right in the end.'

He loved his tractors too, and all the farm machines. He could repair them himself, and liked them to be kept as his tools were. I'd often hear him swearing at the men for their neglect of the machinery. He loved his life, and when sometimes he was vexed, I used to say to him, 'Good heavens, what *is* the matter? You have a perfect life: you're your own master; out in the open air; get off for a spree if you feel like it; plenty of everything, and an endless variety of activities and experiences every day!'

Then he'd laugh and say, 'Well, I suppose you're right; but I wish that blessed potato planter would work. Here we are, held up for want of a part promised months ago.' Or, 'This rain, just as we were getting the combine going! Now we'll have to wait for days,' or, 'The damned sheep have broke out looking for water; if we don't get it soon, I'll pack up. . .' etc.

But if I said, 'I've heard the first cuckoo, or seen the first swallow, or picked the first celandine,' he would be all happiness again.

*   *   *

142

When Harold Tucker died suddenly at the swimming baths, Helen remembered him thus:

HAROLD TUCKER, STARWELL FARM

My friend is dead;
But death was kind to him
And came with foot so soft
And wing so swift
There was no time for fear or cry.
Without a hint whither his soul was bent,
He left us.
He loved the earth he tilled,
The beauty of the red-gold wheat,
The silvery barley and the rustling oats
Filled him with joy.
He loved the grain of wood,
The tools to shape it fitting to his palm
Gave him delight.
He loved small, helpless, tender things,
The pee-wit's nest was sacred to his plough
And the crouched fledgling coloured as the earth
Need not have feared his tread,
So warily he went guessing they were there.
Small flowers he loved,
And when a rare flower came
And grew among the stones
He cherished it as others would a gem.
'Is it your favourite?' I would ask;
'Yes'—and quickly he would add
'But all—all flowers are lovely.'
Childlike his nature was,
And his faults too;
But faults and virtues all
Made up a man beloved.
He was my friend.
We must not, will not mourn;
His soul has reached the bourne
To which we travel painfully.
'All will come right', he used to say.

143

And he was wise, for with him
All is well.

*   *   *

All the time Edward's poetry was becoming more and more widely known and acclaimed. Helen gave talks about him to literary societies, there were programmes on the wireless about his poetry and Mother herself gave a broadcast reading of them from Bristol. There was a radio adaptation of her books—Olive Gregg took the part of Helen—and I remember our wry amusement when we saw the script and noticed that the Kentish postman coming to the door was directed to speak in 'mummerset', a kind of burring motley dialect which in those days served for any rustic speech—as unlike the Kentish intonation as Devon is from Norfolk.

In 1937 Robert Eckert, an American judge, published Edward's biography and bibliography. He had been an admirer of Edward's ever since the time of the Guthrie Pear Tree Press and his fine collection of first editions, letters and manuscripts was given to the Bodleian Library at Oxford on his death. Two years later John Moore published his biography.

Scarcely a week passed without several requests for the use of Edward's poems in English and American anthologies. W. H. Auden wrote of Edward as an early poetic influence. University students wrote for information on his life for Ph.D. theses. His poems were often included in radio broadcasts, and when Patric Dickinson was arranging the first long programme on Edward's poetry for the Third Programme, it was suggested that the job of reading the verse should be given to a persistent young man, fresh from drama school, who had been hoping for broadcasting work for some time and who haunted the studios: 'Oh let's give this fellow Dick Burton a try!' they said; and so it was that Richard Burton, then with some Welsh music still in his voice, was one of the first readers.

While she was at Starwell Farm, Helen's circle of friends was widening even further—admirers perhaps of her two books in the first place, and then of Edward's poetry and prose—Richard Church, John Moore, Lord Horder, Cecil and Jill

Day-Lewis, Thomas Moult, Andrew Young, Vernon Watkins —many of whom she visited and who came to see her at Starwell. Frank Shelley, actor-manager of the Playhouse at Oxford, took her often to plays there, calling for her and bringing her back in his car.

Through reading his book *A Tenement in Soho* and later reading some correspondence about the author, George Thomas, in *The Times*, Helen and he became regular correspondents. He was a London dustman's son and was suffering from muscular dystrophy. He had a passion for reading and there was an appeal in *The Times* to send him books, to which Helen had responded. For several years his wife Mary brought him in his wheel-chair travelling in the guard's van to Chippenham, down to Starwell, and the Tuckers took him for rides through the lush pasture and downland of Wiltshire in their little Austin. Vividly I recall one farm we took him to see: the farmhouse, long and low, of mellowed stone, hung with wisteria, lay back from a long wide drive. On either side of this drive stood an avenue of six great circular wheat-ricks rising on the mushroom-like stone staddles, their conical tops thatched with golden wheat straw, and the slanting edges below the thatch shorn and even, and on the top of each rick a finial in the shape of a three-arched crown made of woven straw. In the golden evening sunlight, a richer or more English scene would be difficult to imagine. In the evenings, when the supper had been cleared away, George and Helen would have long talks about books and then they would take it in turns to read aloud from a novel by Dickens, Hardy or Jane Austen.

Two or three years before the second war a friend of Ian and Dorothy MacAlister, Rowland Watson, came to see Helen. He had been a warm admirer of Edward's work for many years, and particularly of the prose, which he hoped to promote. By coincidence, he and his wife had, in their early married life, lived in the next village to Otford, and though they must have seen Helen on walks, they'd never met socially at that time.

It had been decided to have a memorial to Edward on the hill called the Shoulder of Mutton above Steep where we lived for several years before and during the war. Rowland

Watson was secretary of the memorial committee and did all the work of sending out appeals, choosing the great Sarsen stone from Avebury, and arranging for it to be taken to Steep and set into the hillside, with a bronze plaque bearing Edward's name.

The unveiling of the stone was a marvellous occasion for Helen, the fulfilment of her steady faith, love and hard work in making Edward's poetry more widely known. The ceremony began with trumpeters from the Royal Artillery sounding the Reveille. Her letter to the Hootons tells them about it:

14 October 1937   Starwell Farm
                                                Sheldon, Chippenham
My dears, my very dearest old friends,

You will I expect have seen something of the lovely happenings on 2 October. It was for me a day of days—everything combined to make it perfect—the weather, the beauty of the place, the kindness of everyone and the enthusiasm. I felt overwhelmed and indeed even now I can hardly think of anything else.

Dear old Nevinson said to me in answer to something I said to him 'Yes he would have been amused (apropos Lords and Bishops) but he would have been pleased'. And I am sure he would because of the obvious sincerity of everyone concerned. I have got to know Lord and Lady Horder—the kindest souls possible—I have made real friends there for we 'fell' for each other. It was a great gathering of old friends and after it was all over I had a party at which all could meet and talk and exchange memories of Edward— de la Mare, Jesse Berridge, Duncan Williams, Guthrie, Edward's brothers, MacAlister and lots more names, Lupton among them and the Lushingtons (of the 244th Battery). Masefield and Nevinson both spoke well and Lord Horder's speech was lovely too. The two former especially—of course Nevinson's was of a very personal intimate kind, that of our old and loyal friend. Our little Berryfield has now its tablet and on the Mutton stands an ancient stone from Wiltshire in whose crannies little plants have already begun to grow. In Petersfield Hospital the Bishop dedicated a child's cot with Edward's name over it.

146

I broadcast some of Edward's poems the other day and hope soon to read some again in London. Irene has just been staying here—she often comes. We are fond of each other tho' not awfully congenial. She is a 'boss' and somehow we get on each other's nerves a bit, but she is a great believer in 'the family', tho' I think she thinks me a fool. She cannot read Edward's poems and dislikes my books—not that that matters really but from that you can tell how dissimilar we are—Oh we are in every way almost. She looks very young for her age sixty-four. I am sixty now!

How sweet you are to me, bless you. How I wish we saw something of each other. Old friends are the best, indeed I don't want new friends now. Dear Harry and Janet what days what times we have seen and lived together. All young then! and now we are old. How wonderful life is, how full mine has been. My three grandchildren fill it. I can't love them enough they are so hurtingly dear to me, especially Rosy aged four a little wiry fair haired creature with great round brown eyes and lovely affectionate ways, *very* coy with men whom she adores indiscriminately.

God bless you my dears. Forgive me please do, I don't forget you *ever* but get overwhelmed at times with my cares for my two girls.

My dear love always   Helen

During the Second World War Mother had constant visitors to the farm, often mothers with their children who had come from London to avoid the bombing. Merfyn was by now in the R.A.O.C. and in France, and his wife Zelda with their son Edward, Bronwen, now a young widow for the second time with her son Charles Davidson, and I with my daughter Rosemary stayed for long periods. Aunt Irene also came for a long stay, though she and Mother used to have fierce arguments—they disagreed on almost every subject. Irene, for instance, kept meticulous accounts and at one time tried to show her younger sister how pleasant and satisfying and simple it was to see where your money had gone. Though by now she had long given up trying to get Helen to take this seriously, she would enlist her help at the end of the day when she totted up her expenditure after shopping in Chippenham. There was an occasion when she could not account for a penny halfpenny and they cudgelled their brains as to what it could have been spent on, all to no purpose. Helen was getting bored and impatient and suggested, 'Why not just write down, "Gave H. 1½d." and then we can go on with *Bleak House*?' But Irene was shocked at such flippancy.

Helen had always loved talk: discussion and argument entered into any subject—even if she was not always sure of her ground—with vigour and enthusiasm, as indeed she did in all her activities. She often 'trailed her cloak' with her elder, humourless sister, drawing her into discussions upon subjects they had always disagreed on. Even when we were grown women Bronwen and I became very discomforted, even distressed, at the fierceness of their arguments. But they both enjoyed the fight, never giving way an inch.

EASTBURY

EARLY IN the nineteen fifties, it was felt that Mother and
I should move near to Bronwen and her husband—she had
married, at the beginning of the war, a very old friend from
Otford days—who lived in Berkshire. The three grandchildren
were now in their teens—Charles, Bronwen's son, doing his
National Service in Germany, Rosemary working on a farm,
and Merfyn's boy, Edward, soon to leave school. After much
searching we found the thatched cottage at Eastbury on the
banks of the river Lambourn, a chalk stream under the
Downs, where Mother and I lived for the last thirteen years
of her life. She missed the lush elm-grown fields of Wiltshire,
with the rich hedge-banks of flowers so near, but she soon
learned to love the gentle chalk downs and to find the chalk-
loving rock-roses and many kinds of bell-flowers. The bare
grass of the garden she quickly transformed into flower beds,
shrubs and lawn.

She wrote to Eleanor Farjeon who had helped us with the
deposit for the mortgage on the cottage:

[Summer 1955]   Bridge Cottage
                                               Eastbury

Dearest Eleanor

I have had a letter to you in my mind and heart this many
a day, but time and energy were lacking to get it to my pen's
point. Now your need of knowing about the letters [Edward
Thomas's letters for use in Eleanor's book *Edward Thomas—
The Last Four Years*] and my need of thanking you for
letting me see them creates both and I sit down in the sunshine to write to you.

First of all my blessings most truly in any use you want to
make of these letters. I read them with Oh such interest and
memories crowding in all the time. I was puzzled by one or
two of the references to Frost and wonder what evoked them.
Some mood I suppose of R. F.'s. Only Edward Garnett spot-
ted the value of the poems. Harold Munro years after Edward's death wrote to me a rather grovelling sort of letter
saying in effect that now when others saw their merit his eyes
had been opened too etc. etc. I felt bitter towards him for

what a little praise would have meant to Edward. Except that as for the poems, of these he was sure, in a way he'd never been before about his work and was not put off by the repeated refusal of them. That was wonderful.

How much he relied on you Eleanor for so much of every kind that you gave him. In turning out I have come across dozens and dozens (perhaps hundreds) of my letters to him. I wept to see them so carefully arranged and kept, and do you know I can still remember the writing of some of them— the very time and place and circumstances. My memory works like that, moments of ecstasy of joy or grief are stamped ineradicably on my mind. I could mark the spot and have done so several times in my life years after. God bless you Eleanor yet more than He has already, and preserve your sight to the end of your most wonderfully rich life and being.

As for this cottage which you helped us to buy it shapes into an adorable home. It is a most darling place ancient and gnarled and nooky and cornery and full of character and warmth and of all that life means—life and death and birth and joy and sadness and just the lovely jog trot of the woman who minds it for her folk.

Since we've been here I have been all on my own making it into our abiding place, for Myfanwy is away all day. And this is a job after my own heart. I love contriving and finding places and finding better places and putting our little belongings where they look and serve best. Oh it's been lovely doing it, but I've found it very tiring for I begin to feel my years. But each day brought order to some part where chaos had been and now at last each room has some design and being and character of its own. And I look at my little world and see that it is good. Now it needs our friends to come and warm it and bless it for us. *Please* do come Eleanor, for without your help it could not have been ours. Oh the cost in money I mean! But miraculously we could *just*—only just— do it. I had some BBC windfalls and had saved some money from my book years ago which had increased. And with this and begging and borrowing we just managed it. We remember every day those who helped us and are grateful and happy to have such friends.

My dear love   your Helen

Two years after coming to the Lambourn Valley, Helen had to go to hospital in Guildford, where she underwent painful and exhausting treatment. From there she went on to a nursing home for a while, and returned home completely cured, though exhausted, in time to see her granddaughter Rosemary married, and in the following year, the birth of her first great-grandchildren, twins Zoë and Christopher, a few days after the death of her elder sister Irene.

At about this time Helen wrote to her Wiltshire friend Grace, whom she had known since Grace was in her mid-teens and engaged to Cyril Rice. Grace was one of the family who had found Starwell Farm for her. Now Grace and Cyril had six children of their own, the elder ones getting married. Grace had written asking Helen's thoughts on the hereafter.

Bridge Cottage
Eastbury

Dearest Grace,

Since your letter came I have given much thought as to how to answer you, and I am really no nearer. Because I have no fixed 'belief' I have no beliefs founded on religion, just as I have no religious creed. I am a Christian in the sense that Christ seems to me to be the greatest teacher there has ever been, and the greatest man too and I have tried to model my life on his teaching though I know I have often fallen very short of it. I do not either believe or disbelieve the mystery of his birth, for it does not seem important. It is the most lovely poem that has ever been and as one takes into one's soul the mystery of beauty which poets reveal, so I have rejoiced in that and it has become a part of my being. I only tell you this because there is so much mystery in life and death and the mystery is as much a part of life as what we call reality. Therefore I find it comes naturally to me to feel that in some quite—to me—inconceivable way Edward and I will be reunited when I die. We may not be apart now, and he may have me in a way that I have not him and shall not have 'til death releases my soul and reveals to me truths and states I have no hint of now. I do not call this a belief in after life, I do not believe it with my mind but my heart has had intimations several times of things beyond my reason, beyond my imagination and I have felt that for a flash of a second some deep truth and hope and joy has been revealed to me but I could not say what it is, only I know a great joy has invaded my spirit. I cannot say more than this, dear Grace. All life—birth, living, love, doing and being is *such* a mystery I certainly cannot believe that death is the end. That seems to me a sort of blasphemy.

It is lovely to me dear Grace to know that you have found something in me to remember and brood over and that our lives came together as they did is wonderful to me. Without it I should not have come back to Wiltshire and renewed my spirit among those fields and those elms and friends. Forgive me if I write no more. My sight is so bad I can hardly see my pen making marks and I hope you can read it.

God bless you always and my love always.   your Helen

Helen's proudest moment as a girl had been when her father wrote to her, 'Nellie, you are the Queen of Letter Writers'—and in addition to her long letters to friends, she began writing memories of her childhood and recalling some of those she had met and distant scenes from her life with Edward which had not come into her two published books.

A close friendship developed between Helen and Joy Finzi, widow of the composer Gerald Finzi, a friendship which brought her much happiness, particularly in talks of books and people. One of Helen's favourite writers was Thomas Hardy and Gerald Finzi had set a great many of his poems to music. Joy also took Helen to concerts by the Newbury String Players, now conducted by Christopher Finzi. They went to the theatre in Oxford and Stratford—the Stratford visits were highlights of the year and I remember how entranced Helen was by David Warner's *Hamlet*. It was Joy too who arranged for the recording of Helen's reading of Edward's poems. It was made by two young men who had recorded many of the Finzi concerts and were anxious to try the spoken word. Helen was now eighty-seven. The first of two recordings made in our Eastbury cottage was a failure. The clock ticked, the Swindon bus and several race-horse transporters roared past, our old spaniel Sophie snored and the typed pages being slid off sounded like a water-sluice.

By the time a second recording could be arranged, Helen's sight had deteriorated so that she spoke many of the poems from memory. A record was eventually made from the tape-recording and copies of it have gone all over the world. When Helen heard of Merfyn's sudden death soon after his retirement from motor journalism later that year, she was very quiet and still. By then Bronwen had come to be her very near neighbour—Merfyn had been an affectionate and reliable son, but his visits were rare—and so her two daughters gave her what comfort they could. She still enjoyed seeing her granddaughter Rosemary and her husband Douglas, who walked with their four children over the fields to see her at weekends from the next village. Bronwen then had two grandchildren, and Merfyn two also, and Helen delighted in watching the children's hands to see if they bore any of the strength and beauty of their great-grandfather.

Up to the last year of her life Helen was able to read, which was her greatest pleasure. Her enthusiasms were Shakespeare —and books about him—Keats, Hardy, Dickens, the Brontës, Jane Austen. She read them again and again, often aloud in the evenings. The last book she read aloud was *Our Mutual Friend*, our favourite. She read avidly books of history, especially biographies of her heroes, Nelson and Queen Elizabeth. She loved Churchill's *History of the English Speaking Peoples*— 'What a man—what a writer!'—and had a particular affection for Lord David Cecil's books on Cowper and Jane Austen. She enjoyed Max Beerbohm's essays and broadcasts—her ringing laughter at his humour ending with a sigh of nostalgic pleasure.

The last twelve years of her life in Berkshire were rich in friends and books. Joy Finzi and Mary Dawson took her over the country in their cars, and to the theatre in Oxford. Many old and new friends came to Eastbury to visit her and the cottage sitting room was lively with talk and laughter. One of her friends, who first came to see her in 1960, Terence Cooper, visited her several times each year, and they exchanged long letters. These letters, from which the following extracts are given with Terence's permission, show better than any words of mine her vitality of mind and spirit while her arthritis made her more and more housebound and her sight was failing.

Helen's love of the natural world was as keen as ever.

'The hedge in the garden is full of snowdrops. This valley is a very snowdroppy place and they grow wild and are very lovely. The aconites—a special favourite of mine—I can't get to do well here. At my farm in Wiltshire which I wish you'd seen they spread and flowered directly after Christmas, I could see their sunny little bubbles from my window. But it was a most lovely land for flowers. I miss most deeply the rich hedgebanks full of primroses and violets and cowslips—every sort of flower for every season, and bluebells and foxgloves in the woods. Oh it was heavenly country for trees and flowers and in this chalk country I miss terribly the richness which that rich land produced. In the fields of the farm I knew every inch and could go at once to pick crab apple blossom, and I knew the beautiful bush of pussy willow and in the wood a very early wild plum. And teazles and great thistles—a rare kind most beautiful that I knew where to look for each year. About a mile from the house by a stream I found wild aconites half in and half out of the water and great buxom kingcups.'

'On Friday I actually did a bit of gardening and enjoyed having my hands in contact with the earth, and though my wretched knee protested all the way I did not regret my hour or two of my favourite occupation. But now the cruel dead weather has come back and I am housebound and bored and a fine old misery, and very ashamed at my failure to count my blessings.'

'A sight of a cedar gives me great joy in its dark dignity and its "layers of shade" and its aloofness and yet something in its solitariness and beauty strike a deep response in me. I could easily have been a tree worshipper.'

'A good deal of the beloved English scene is no longer visible to me, but I have seen it and known it and loved it and if I can't see the reddening willows and the thickening tops of the elms I *know* they are there and that Spring is coming. A kind friend took me to see the snowdrops in Welford Park and when I got out of the car and bent down I could see not only drifts and drifts of snowdrops, but glowing patches of hardy cyclamens, pink and mauve among their ornamental leaves and pools reflecting the bright sunlight of aconites.'

'Oh these lovely mild Autumn days, when leaves just sleepily flutter off the branch. The garden is a blank for the first time since the snow went, but the snowberries are pretty and some plants came with full rye corn stalks to pack them, and the sheaf is in the courtyard and the tits are round it and bend the straws over as they flutter and perch and peck at the heads of grains. If only it would get warmer. My old heart has to work so hard to keep me going in these cold days, and I puff and pant with every movement.'

*   *   *

As long as she was able to get out, Helen remained a passionate theatre-goer.

'Last night I ventured as far as Oxford to see *Who's Afraid of Virginia Woolf* and I could see enough to make it intelligible and the play impressed me very much, though I could not help thinking that its blatancy was overdone. But I suppose that is the American way, and certainly provided an experience I am glad not to have missed, and I still think of it and try to sort out my ideas about it as an artistic whole. Some of the dialogue is so utterly crude and schoolboyish and I find it perplexing to assess it. You have probably seen it and I should like to know how it impressed you. We are going to see *Phedre* by Racine soon. I enjoy the theatre now more than ever and if in the front row can see well enough not to be quite lost.'

'The ballet was an unforgettable experience. Being in that vast historic theatre was a thrill in itself. It was packed and there was a distinguished guest [President Nehru] in the Royal

Box. Our seats were perfect and the second ballet *Les Biches* was a glorious and light hearted affair gay and lively which set one's expectation and eagerness for the final climax of Fonteyn and Nureyev in *Bayardere*. They of course exceeded all that had gone before in their grace and dexterity and superhuman movements. One was left wondering did I really see that or am I dreaming. Such perfect dual motion as if the two bodies became as one and with such effortless (so it seemed) grace. At the end they were called more than a dozen times for it was their last appearance together this season and it was very exciting to be with that terrific applause and appreciation.'

'As for *Peter Grimes* it was an experience I was glad to have had. But though the sea element was impressive I was not moved by any of it. I could not hear one word of the libretto, and none of the music lingers in the memory. There are no arias and beyond the great massive sound I remember no details. I sat near the flutes and was fascinated by the way they came in as the sea birds. I wish I could appreciate Britten's music, for music is a great soother and comforter— but I can't. I cannot transmute those strange discords and harsh sounds without harmony or melody to any spiritual essence or heart warming comfort. My lack of intellect is a hindrance to adventuring into the arts I cannot for the life of me comprehend. My mind has lost what elasticity it ever had. This I am pleased to note in reading *Conversations with Max* I shared with that delightful creature, whose taste including a dislike of Shaw's work was so often my own.'

*   *   *

She continued to feel the loss of her husband and to champion his poetry.

'I had a bitter disappointment which I tried not to let appear, to mar the happiness of the family. Some time ago Fabers wrote me a long and enthusiastic letter telling me they were issuing a selection of E's poems with an introduction by R. S. Thomas. Then later they wrote to say that R. S. T. would like to dedicate the little volume to me and I was up in the sky, for every new issue of the poems is good for spreading further E.T.'s work. And that you know is the dearest object to my heart. Well just before Christmas they wrote that it had been decided not to include E.T. in the new paper back selection of poets. He was to be left out. The implication is obvious. They no longer feel that E.T. will sell. I cannot express what I felt and indeed I go on feeling and wondering and despairing. I wrote at once to them. But after all they are business people. But I'm sick at heart and don't really want to go on living if Edward's poems are going to sink into oblivion. For the growing-up public on which a poet's reputation depends will forget his name unless the publishers loyally keep him in print. Because the poems are so characteristic, they give me the man and I long for his sake that they become part of the English poetic heritage. I'm not a critic. I cannot use the critic's vocabulary. But people who *can* have spoken of them with great praise and I passionately want them to live. This disappointment is quite in the tradition of his life and suffering.' [Not long after, the publishers changed their minds and the volume has now gone into several impressions.]

'How I love meeting and listening to those people far above me in learning and enlarging my experiences. I'm very fortunate in knowing and being loved by people whom I admire and whose minds stir my own feeble one and give it new life. Oh that is the terrible thing that I lost with Edward. His wonderful mind which he was always willing and eager to give to me. But I've only plodded on as best I could with no help no leader or guide to great writing and as I say there are great gaps in my knowledge and understanding. I have not really grown up yet.'

*   *   *

She felt the onset of age with its deprivations, and for comfort her thoughts turned back to the natural world.

'I have been so wretchedly poorly, and am still in bed. My heart is playing me up and makes me utterly hopeless.

157

However it does not rob me of my power of imagination and the happiness of those I love I can still enter into and share. And I am very happy indeed to think of you on your beloved downs and Pewsey Vale, and as I lie in bed here kicking so against the pricks, I have been re-creating some of my hours of utter content and joy and fulfilment with my beloved striding along untiringly, he reading the scene as a book and telling me sometimes what he saw and heard, but often silent. And I trying to learn from him so that my experience of all that beauty and mystery might match his own and bring me closer to him.'

'This is only a note to tell you of the sudden death of my son Merfyn while on a visit to his stepson in Germany. It was sudden and painless. We are a close knit family and he was most beloved. We did not see him often, but his visits were always occasions of joy, and he was here for a few most happy hours on my birthday in July. He and his wife Zelda were most happy together and she brings him home today. Bronny and Myfanwy will go to the funeral. He had just retired and was enjoying it. The mystery of life oppresses me. If only I had gone instead.'

'I myself do not fear death. I used to, and Claudio's vision [in *Measure for Measure*] of becoming a handful of dust blown about the universe would have turned me rigid with fear. But not now. To mingle with the earth, to nourish the roots of a hawthorn bush—that most British of ancient trees —to misquote Edward—seems to me now most desirable. Everything about the hawthorn bush is lovable, the bitter sweet scent of its flowers who for all they are not perfectly white, yet give the semblance of snow to the late spring bushes, so closely packed, so crowding to the sun and even on the leaves too, which children call bread-and-cheese and eat with relish, or used to when relish was a quality people felt. The tough wood, dark outside and contorted by the winds on which it thrives, is red inside. No wood so good to burn crackle and roar and re-kindle at a breath from the embers.'

*　　　　*　　　　*

Towards the autumn of 1966 the arthritis in Helen's back and hips made bed the most desirable place and many friends came to see her to talk or to read aloud. Her greatest sorrow was to be out of physical touch with the earth, the garden which she loved to work in. In March 1967 she wrote,

Unfortunately, I am not awfully well and cannot help feeling very often very depressed, in spite of the lovely sunshine which floods my room. I often have my window open and can listen to the birds, and wonder if I shall ever again be at as close quarters to them.

Earlier in the year, from her bed, Helen gave two long interviews for BBC radio programmes—for it was coming up to the fiftieth anniversary of Edward's death at Arras on 9 April 1917, and there were to be several tributes to his memory. One of the interviews was with Professor R. George Thomas of University College Cardiff, whom she had met several times when he was editing Edward's letters to Gordon Bottomley, and who, she felt, had a deep insight into Edward's character and work. It gave her great contentment to think that he would be preparing a definitive volume of the poems and eventually a biography.

She listened to these broadcasts about Edward with a detached repose, and three days later, gently and quietly drifted from us, to join him after their long parting.

I have not 'set the table on a roar', but I have embraced every aspect of life passionately, that is the best you can say of me. My book in a little has helped Edward's reputation, and he is now among the immortals.

PHOTOGRAPH ALBUM

1

2

3

4

7

8

9

11

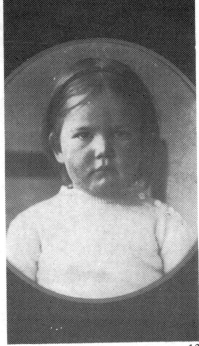

10

12

13

14

15

16

17

18